Hard **WORDS**
for *Interesting Times*

Hard **WORDS**
for *Interesting Times*

Biblical texts in contemporary contexts

John L. Bell

WILD GOOSE PUBLICATIONS

www.ionabooks.com

First published 2003 by
Wild Goose Publications, Fourth Floor, Savoy House,
140 Sauchiehall Street, Glasgow G2 3DH, UK,
the publishing division of the Iona Community.
Scottish Charity No. SCO03794.
Limited Company Reg. No. SCO96243.

ISBN 1 901557 75 8

Cover © Graham Maule, 2003

A catalogue record for this book is available from the British Library.

Overseas distribution
Australia: Willow Connection Pty Ltd, Unit 4A,
3-9 Kenneth Road, Manly Vale, NSW 2093.
New Zealand: Pleroma, Higginson Street,
Otane 4170, Central Hawkes Bay.

Permission to reproduce any part of this work in Australia
or New Zealand should be sought from Willow Connection.

Printed by Bell & Bain, Thornliebank, Glasgow

Contents

Introduction

The chapters in this book were never intended for publication, or for reading.

One chapter was adapted from a lecture, the others are reconstructed sermons. And, though some may disagree, I do not believe that either of these forms is meant to be read; they are meant to be 'delivered'.

Although that is the proper term, its curiosity is rarely noticed. The more common use of the verb 'to deliver' pertains to birthing a child – an experience I have never had. But I suppose that in an analogous way, if apprehension and excitement, pain and relief are part and parcel of birthing a child, they also play their part in conceiving and delivering a sermon.

These chapters cannot replicate the searching of the deliverer's mind for words and illustrations appropriate to the peculiar situation and particular congregation for which the original speech was intended. Nor can endless dots or parentheses imitate the ebb and flow, the emphasis and understatement that make preaching an event in which the speaker interacts with the congregation.

But if the chapters convey some of the fascination that the Bible increasingly holds for the author, and if they convey something of how critical it is to hold on to the hard words of God so that faith may deepen and the planet survive, perhaps that will be enough.

All material was delivered between 1999 and 2002 in a variety of locations on both sides of the Atlantic. In these years the interrelatedness of the world has become all too transparent as our knowledge of global ecology and global terrorism has troubled our consciences.

Because such things threaten the world God made and the people created in God's image, the Christian faith must address such troubled times. Otherwise it is not Christian faith but an escapist ideology. I hope and pray that what is written here may contribute to such a response and that the original midwife whose name is God may deliver us from every evil.

John L. Bell

April 2003

Acknowledgements

I express my indebtedness to the churches and venues whose invitations to speak lie behind the chapters in this book, and in particular to the English Reformed Church in the Begijnhof, Amsterdam and Greenbelt Festival whose peoples have encouraged my journey and stretched my faith for over two decades.

I also thank Sandra Kramer, the publishing manager of Wild Goose Publications, for her tireless attention to detail in editing raw manuscript and for providing helpful suggestions to ameliorate my worst infelicities.

And, as with all that I have ever published, my gratitude to my colleague, Graham Maule, can never be overstated. Without his encouragement, management, and artistic and seminal thinking, little that bears my name would ever see the light of day.

1 Love does

Texts: 1 Corinthians 13; Mark 7:24–30

Love is patient and kind.

PAUL

I have never really liked Paul. He's much too protestant – too exact, too dogmatic, too systematic in his theology, too keen to avoid loopholes, too introvert, too humourless.

Mary and Peter are much more rounded figures, much more untidy, much more gregarious, much more catholic.

But Paul ... I imagine that in heaven there will be a queue of male comedians and angry women outside Paul's door.

The men will shout up to his window: 'Are you the Paul who sent a letter to the Corinthians?' and when he shyly says 'Yes', they'll roar, 'Did you ever get a reply?'

And the women – the angry women – they'll want to see what kind of mother he had who turned him against the opposite sex.

I suppose many people might use a contemporary psychological term to describe Paul. They might say that he was a left-brain thinker.

LEFT-BRAIN CORINTHIANS

You know about the right brain/left brain stuff?

It is reckoned that the left brain, which governs the right-hand side of our body, is the part of us that thinks very logically. It is ordered, mathematical, analytical, good at thinking through an argument.

The right sphere of the brain, on the other hand, is said to be more creative, more imaginative, more given to fantasy ...

You decide *whom* you'll marry with your right brain. It is never a logical choice. It's not a matter of going through an address book and eliminating or choosing a candidate according to predetermined criteria. Romance comes into it and deep feeling.

But you decide *when* you'll get married with your left brain. You have to be certain it is a suitable day. You'll want to be sure that you're not booked in to have open-heart surgery that afternoon.

Paul strikes us as a cool, logical, cautious left-brain thinker, not given to fancy language or poetry. Anyone who has tried to set Paul to music knows that. Can you imagine what tune would go with these words which appear early on in his letter to the Corinthians?

> *'To the unmarried and to widows I say this:*
> *it is a good thing if like me they stay as they are;*
> *but if they do not have self-control, they should marry.*
> *It is better to be married than to burn with desire.'*

It doesn't exactly rhyme. It doesn't inspire a romantic

melody. But that is what Paul tends to be like – slightly legalistic, proscriptive, even dull sometimes – until ...

RIGHT-BRAIN CORINTHIANS

... until we come to 1 Corinthians 13 where, for reasons we do not know, Paul begins to use his right brain and bursts into pure poetry – poetry so profound that many people of my age and older would have been expected, in childhood, to commit it to memory:

'Though I speak with the tongues of men and of angels and have not charity, I am become as sounding brass or a tinkling cymbal; and though I understand all mysteries and have all knowledge, if I have not charity, I am nothing.'

(We learned it in the English of King James at my school. If that was good enough for Jesus, it was good enough for us!)

In this poem, there are words that evoke noise ...

'a sounding brass, a clanging symbol'

There are words that conjure up pictures ...

'now we see puzzling reflections in a mirror'

And there are very evocative lines that we might want to chew over ...

'when I was a child I spoke, I thought, I understood as a child'

There are no long sentences with contorted thought. Everything is almost epigrammatic, reaching a positive climax at the beginning of the second paragraph:

'love is patient, love is kind'

DOWNHILL CORINTHIANS

But from that positive assertion, Paul seems to change direction, to turn negative:

'Love envies NO ONE
is NEVER boastful,
NEVER conceited,
NEVER rude;
Love is NEVER selfish,
NEVER quick to take offence.
Love keeps NO score of WRONGS,
takes NO pleasure in the SINS of others.'

Oh Paul ... just when the muse was upon you, why did you nosedive into the negative? Why does your paean, your hymn of praise about love, need to wallow in the NOTS and the NEVERS? Why not keep to the right brain – just once?

But Paul is quite correct, for love is not simply a matter of intuition, it is also a matter of choice. Love is not simply about following the dominant emotion, it is also about exercising sensitivity and choice.

Love is both right- and left-brain. It has to do with the romantic but also with the rational. It has to do with feelings, but also with fairness. It is passionate, but it is also perceptive.

CREATIVE DISCIPLINE

When a composer is infatuated with a musical idea which buzzes about his head and will not give him peace, it does not remain shapeless.

He has to decide on a key, he has to decide on a structure, he has to think about which instruments might play the piece or which voices might sing it.

Do these decisions limit his passionate idea? No, they allow the idea to be refined and communicated to others.

When a poet feels inspired by a particular thought, she has to think about words to express it, about length of verses, about rhyme and suitable vocabulary.

Does this limit her creativity? No, it allows the passionate idea to be expressed intelligibly.

So when Paul, in the middle of his passionate enthusiasm for love, begins to outline some caveats and suggest guidelines, it is not to spoil the fun. It is to enable the marvel and mystery of love to be communicated and understood.

Love is both right- and left-brain – both passion and logic, both romance and reason.

IS LOVE BLIND?

To claim that love is blind and that is the way it should be is to fail to deal with reality.

We all know, don't we, parents who have been so devoted to their children that rather than let them become independent adults, they have smothered the uniqueness in them. Love them – oh yes, they have loved them, but there has been no objectivity, no sensitivity to what would help the children to grow. No willingness to let go.

And we may know couples whose relationship has been stormy, and the storms have never been resolved. Sometimes the rows are caused by the jealousy of the one, sometimes by the possessiveness of the other.

Then one day they announce: 'We'll get married and it will be all right.'

No, no. They'll get married and it will be all wrong.

They might love each other – but if it is all romance and no reasoning, if it's all feeling and no thinking, then their marriage will be doomed.

When our love is something that involves decision-making, choice, not just going on how we feel, then that is a love which makes a difference.

I know that and so might you, so the story that follows may resonate with your own experience.

PASSING A REAL PEACE

About five years ago I went to the Roman Catholic Church of St Augustine in Washington, DC.

It is an African–American congregation – the church is about 98% black. There I had one of the most profound worship experiences of my life. It was partly to do with the magnificent music, partly to do with the profound silence, partly to do with the insightful and direct preaching, but also something else.

During mass, as happens in Catholic churches, people passed the peace. And I watched as a tall black man in his early 30s, who was sitting about seven rows in front of me, walked along each of the rows and shook people by the hand, and patted children on the head, and looked kindly on everyone.

And then he came to me – obviously a stranger in the church – and he smiled and he said,

The peace of the Lord Jesus Christ be with you.
And I am so glad that you came to our church this morning.'

I found myself unable to speak, but I remember thinking,

'Who am I to have this honour? My ancestors transported millions of your ancestors as slaves across the Atlantic Ocean. And you wish me the peace of Christ, and welcome me into your church when you could have thought I was just another curious white guy come to see the circus.'

Obviously the gospel of love he believed in was about more than feeling – it was about deciding to forgive; it was about building new bonds, not being shackled to old prejudices.

JESUS AND REAL LOVING

It certainly wouldn't have been Paul, but it might have been a woman who reminded Jesus that love was not just feelings but also choices and decisions – right- and left-brain.

The woman in question appears in Matthew's Gospel not long after Jesus has spoken about turning the other cheek and loving your enemy. She is a Canaanite, not a Jew, and she has a daughter whom she desperately wants to be healed, and Jesus doesn't feel like it.

He gives her the party line that he was sent primarily to the Jews and that he shouldn't throw what was meant for the children of Israel to the 'dogs' – a popular slang term for Canaanites.

But the woman is not going to take no for an answer. So she throws the words back in Jesus' face, and reminds Jesus of what he has said before about the outcast and the unwanted, and about doing good, and serving the least.

And Jesus, having heard this woman, changes his mind and heals her child; and in the process he shows that love is not just about what we feel, it is about the choices we make and the decisions we make to show that love in action.

Maybe it was the Canaanite woman who helped Jesus decide to accept the cross, for Jesus did not go to the cross because he felt like it.

Jesus accepted the cross as a matter of conviction and decision. For only thus could humanity see that love is not just about what you feel. It's about what you do.

2 The still, small voice of contradiction

Texts: 1 Kings 19:1–18; Matthew 14:22–33

> *The Word of the Lord came to*
> *him: 'Why are you here, Elijah?'*

TALES FROM CHILDHOOD

Stories – especially the ones we hear in childhood – stay with us all our lives ...

Each of us carries inside the memory of stories our parents or grandparents told us about our family history – the strange people, the funny people. Some of us may remember the first storybook we had at school – when we were five or six. Most of us will remember storybooks we read as we moved through childhood.

And depending on when we grew up and where we grew up, our favourite story from childhood may have been written by Mark Twain or Enid Blyton or Chinua Achebe or Hans Christian Andersen.

Many of us will also remember stories from the Bible, and if we first heard them in childhood, it is possible that our recollection of them will be very limited and our understanding of their meaning perhaps non-existent.

If I were to mention the name Goliath, most of us would think of David killing him. We wouldn't think of the role David's brothers played in the story; we might not remember

King Saul's part in the tale. We would probably have no idea of what a boy of twelve was doing on a battlefield.

And if someone were to say that the story of David and Goliath was in the Bible to show the futility of sophisticated weaponry to defend a nation, we might call that person an idiot. Or if someone were to claim that the story is about how the solutions of one generation don't work in the hands of the next generation, we would similarly find the suggestion very odd.

We may know the story but, because we heard it in childhood, we forget the details and we never ask what it means.

Yet the stories in the Bible, especially the Old Testament, were never intended simply for children. They were meant for adults, and they were chosen for inclusion because they have a much more profound significance than tales produced primarily for children.

THE FAMILIAR STORY

I say this because I feel as if I am only just beginning to understand the story of Elijah on the mountain, although I have heard it, and you may have heard it, many times.

I suppose I could preach about the importance of going somewhere remote to spend time with God. I have heard preachers speak of this before in relation to this story and I have no doubt that it is important sometimes to get away from the noise of the world and be alone with God.

In English such an experience is called a retreat. Sometimes I go on them, sometimes I lead them. Every year thousands of people come for a retreat to the remote island of Iona off the West Coast of Scotland. And when you listen to them, they will tell you of how they went to a deserted beach or to the north end of the island or how – like Elijah – they climbed the hill and became aware of the presence of God and felt deeply blessed. And it could not have happened if they had stayed at home.

I could preach about the importance of retreats – but somehow I don't think that is what this story is about.

Or I could talk about silence – about how God comes to us in silence – because I have heard preachers say that kind of thing before. And I have listened to wise men and wise women talking about the need to shut off the noise from our ears and breathe deeply and feel not for God above us but for God within us.

And I believe that God does meet us in silence and that we should not avoid silence, but I don't think this story is just about silence.

Indeed I fear that I may upset people when I suggest that, far from this being a comforting story in which Elijah was blessed, it is a disturbing story about how God refused to give Elijah what he wanted.

THE FORGOTTEN STORY

Maybe it will become clearer when we look at the parts of the story we forget.

You see, Elijah wasn't going on a deliberate spiritual retreat. He was running away. He had just won a competition devised

21

to see which god was real – the god called Baal, or the God of Israel.

It was a simple competition. Two altars were built and a dead bull was put on each altar. Then nine hundred prophets of Baal prayed and shouted for their god to light the fire and burn the offering. But nothing happened.

When it was Elijah's turn, he said a very simple prayer, the wood burst into flame and the sacrifice was burned. Clearly the real God was on Elijah's side. So he took the nine hundred prophets and killed them, and fearing that the king and queen might not be too pleased, he made a quick getaway – and this is the point in the story where unusual things are said.

The first unusual thing is said by God:

a)   Elijah is asked by God what he's doing sitting in a cave by himself on a mountain. And when God asks the question (and God asks the same question twice – 'WHY ARE YOU HERE?') there is a note of annoyance in God's voice.

The scholars tell us that this question is similar to that asked when God looks for Adam and Eve in the garden after they have tasted forbidden fruit, and God says 'Where are you?'

In both cases God makes it clear from the question that the people being spoken to should not be where they are.

b)   The second unusual thing is Elijah's answer:

He has begun by giving a testimony to self-righteousness – 'I AM HERE BECAUSE OF MY FAITH.' He believes that he is being persecuted for doing good.

And then he tells a downright lie. He says that in the whole country he is the only person who is a real believer.

We know this is a lie because ten minutes later God tells Elijah about seven thousand people who have similarly been faithful but whom – inadvertently – Elijah forgot.

So this story is not simply about a humble believer going on a silent retreat. It's about somebody who has got himself into deep water, blames it on God and claims that he is the only person in society who cares.

So what happens? What happens is that Elijah doesn't get what he wants.

He is on the mountain for the third time in forty-eight hours. And he is on the mountain because for him, as for other Jews, the mountain is the place where God reveals himself. God dramatically lit the altar and burned the bull on the mountain, so maybe God will do something spectacular again. Maybe God will give Elijah a religious fix – to compensate for his bad luck.

So a wind comes ... and Elijah expects God to be in the wind. The wind, after all, circulated on the waters at the creation and God was there. The wind blew the waters of the Red Sea apart to let the Hebrew slaves escape from their Egyptian captors – and God was there.

Plenty of wind ... no God.

And then there is an earthquake. And Elijah feels sure God will be doing this just for him, because when Moses met God on the mountain, the earth shook. There is a lot of shaking ... but no God.

And then there's fire. And how Elijah's heart must have leapt. God, after all, had spoke in fire at the burning bush. God was present in the pillar of fire which guided the Hebrews through the desert. And hadn't God just recently sent fire from heaven to prove that he was the authentic deity?

Plenty of fire, no God.

And then,
and then,
and then ...
nothing.

God is not supposed to do this! God is supposed to be present and active and demonstrative when a paid up prophet needs some reassurance. God should show up in the usual ways when faithful people, whom God has helped before, need a hand.

Wind ... earthquake ... fire ... all the celestial *son et lumière* you ever craved for, but no God.

And then the opposite of what Elijah wanted and expected: in the middle of a pregnant silence, Elijah hears God.

And what does Elijah hear in that silence? Is it a voice which says, 'You are my beloved son in whom I am well pleased?'

No. It is a voice that seems to be singularly unimpressed with Elijah's show of piety. It is a voice that says, 'Go back into the city which you are running away from. I have work for you there.'

WHAT DOES IT ALL MEAN?

So what, then, does this story mean for us, if it is not simply a reminder of the importance of taking a retreat and listening for God in silence. I want to suggest two things:

1) The first is a public and contentious issue.

Elijah tries to be with God on the mountain but God sends him back to the city to find allies who will deal with the abundant corruption there.

Judaism and Christianity are urban faiths. The Bible may begin in a garden, but much of it concerns the life and inhabitants of cities, whether they be Jerusalem or Babylon or Rome or Corinth or Ephesus. And it is cities much more than mountains that make people despair, because in cities we become aware of being at the mercy of powers we cannot control – financial powers, corporate powers, political powers, the powers of consumerist persuasion, controlled by companies who are accountable to no government, but to shareholders whose primary interest is profit.

I was in a city two weekends ago – in Birmingham. I was speaking at a conference of Roman Catholic lay leaders. During one session, a woman in her early fifties stood up and began to ask a question which clearly caused her to tap into emotionally fraught experience.

She has two girls to raise and no husband, so money is tight. The elder daughter is 14 and, like most teenagers, she watches television, buys teenage magazines and has convinced herself that there is a range of commodities she needs to purchase in order to be one of the crowd – CD ROMs, the latest teen fashions, make-up ... you know the kind of thing.

This woman loves her daughter, but she cannot afford what her daughter says she needs to be chic, 'with it' … 'in' … and the mother doesn't know what to do. She feels victimised and alone.

As she spoke, I noticed that of the other three hundred people in the room, a good many were nodding their heads. They too were the parents of children who are increasingly the targets of fashion and media industries run by men my age and older. They too feel helpless in dealing with the demands for this commodity or that commodity which their child says is essential for contemporary teenage living.

And I began to wonder whether Christians are simply going to be victims of this rampant commercialism – or whether there are a lot of people in the city who, together, might confront this idolatry which is as pernicious in the 21st century as it was during the time of Elijah. The only difference is that today our 'gods' do not have foreign-sounding names like 'Baal'. They are much more personable – Adidas, McDonald, Calvin Klein.

I am encouraged in this regard by a book called *The American Paradox* written by David Myers, a world-famous psychologist and a member of the Reformed Church of America.

In analysing the helplessness that people feel in the face of the urban gods they try to flee from, Myers gives examples of how in the '40s, '50s '60s and '70s consistent public pressure against everything from the vilification of black people to the portrayal of violence on television made a significant impact. And his conviction is that rather than run away from the challenge of confronting the urban gods, you should take them on in the company of others and stop feeling like a victim.

The same kind of sentiment is expressed in the affirmation of Alan Boesak, one of the leaders in the struggle to end apartheid in South Africa.

It is not true – he says –
that we are the victims of powers beyond our control.

This is true:
unto us a child is born
and unto us a son is given
and he shall have the authority of government on his
shoulder.

Perhaps this story of Elijah is meant in this century to embolden us, as God's people, to take on the urban gods.

2) My other suggestion is much more personal.

It is simply that, if we take this story and the experience of Elijah seriously, we have to be prepared for the fact that God will not always give us what we want.

Elijah expected God to respect his devotion; God asked him why he had withdrawn. Elijah wanted to escape; he was told to go back to the city. Elijah wanted God to give an exotic display of divine power; he was given an experience of silence.

God does not always give us what we want.

We have to deal with that on Iona, especially when people come for a retreat hoping that they can forget about the marriage problem or the money problem or the personal dilemma which they have left behind in Seattle or London or Glasgow. After three or four days on a remote Hebridean island, the thing they were avoiding comes back into view. And they don't get the warm spiritual glow they were hoping for. They get the jolt or the wake-up call or the encouragement to confront what they are running away from.

That is not what they want. Yet that is what they get, because God, like the best father, the best mother, distinguishes between what is wanted and what is needed.

A child may want chocolate for dinner, but if his mother gives him broccoli … is that a sign of a lack of love?

A child may want, for the third time in the week, to go to the cinema, but if the father says, 'Go and play with your bike in the park' … is that a sign of a lack of love?

A child may throw a tantrum and run to her bedroom, slamming the doors. And if the parents don't follow quickly saying, 'What's the matter, what's the matter?' … is that a lack of love?

Rather, is it not that, for the maturing of the child, the parent differentiates between what she or he wants and what she or he really needs?

Sometimes that will be encouragement
and sometimes contradiction;
sometimes smooth words
and sometimes hard words;
sometimes embrace
and sometimes silence.

And if this fails to persuade, then remember what happened to Peter when in the middle of a gale he tried to walk on water and nearly drowned.

We don't read that Jesus comforted him. We don't read that
Jesus said,
> There, there now, Peter.

We do read that Jesus said,
> What were you scared of?
> Where's your faith?

It was not what Peter wanted to hear but it was maybe what
Peter needed to hear.

For God may at times be silent, but God is never soft.

3 Midwifery for pensioners

Texts: Genesis 17:15–22; Luke 1:5–22

> *How can I be sure of this?*
> *I am an old man and my*
> *wife is well on in years.*

Bing Crosby has begun.

I heard him in Habitat on Friday.

It was pouring with rain in Buchanan Street, but inside the store Bing was singing that sleigh bells were ringing and in the lane snow was glistening.

It always seems a bit odd to me that Americans should dream of one-horse open sleighs in their streets. Such is their obsession with the motorcar that anyone who rides a bicycle, never mind on a sleigh, is considered to be subversive!

It used to be that the seasonal celebrations started in December, around the time when Advent begins, but because of the commercial potential of Christmas it seems as if the season begins a day earlier each year.

In the USA – from which much of our Christmas culture is imported – there is now a constant run of celebration from Hallowe'en, an enormous event in itself, through Thanksgiving into Christmas ... virtually a three-month orgy of seasonal consumerism.

But that is not really what I want to talk about. I leave the financial implications of this time of year to someone else. What I want to do is to take an objective look at the seasons of Advent and Christmas and at what they are essentially about.

I do so because, in addition to the commercialisation of the season, it seems that since the Victorian era there has been a dumbing down, a sentimentalising of what God was doing when he got embroiled with humanity through the incarnation.

THE REAL INCARNATION

Indeed I wonder sometimes whether our understanding of the incarnation isn't more informed by songs like *Away In A Manger* than by a healthy grasp of the stories as they present themselves to us in the Bible.

You see, the one thing which Christmas is not ... is a babyfest.

Yes, there is a baby, and he is laid in a manger. But, if it does not seem too disrespectful to say so, he has a relatively small part. He does nothing. Other people do things for him. He goes nowhere; other people visit him. Furthermore, those among whom he appears are not his own age, nor are they little children.

While I would not for a moment want to devalue school and Sunday school Advent plays for which children may even now be rehearsing, I would want to say that Jesus was not born in a kindergarten or a crèche surrounded by infants whose life experience was limited to being looked after by parents.

But it is infinitely more sentimentally fulfilling to watch

four- and five-year-olds stumble through their lines in a nativity play than to take stock of how old the original cast actually was.

I discovered this recently in Southwark Cathedral in London, where my colleagues and I were running a conference for the Anglican diocese. It was about preparing for Advent. So I began the afternoon by asking people to name all the folk who appear in the Advent and Christmas stories. One by one the names appeared:

Jesus
Mary
Joseph
Shepherds
Wise Men
and then:
Zaccharaiah
Elizabeth
Simeon
Anna
and then:
Herod
Caesar Augustus
Quirinius, the Governor of Syria

(and in case anybody is thinking that I've missed out the innkeeper ... there isn't one. At least, not in the Bible. Nor is there a donkey – not even a little donkey – but don't tell Bing Crosby that. It would upset the Habitat sales).

When we had all these names up, I said to the audience, 'What do these people have in common?'

Do you know what they have in common?

... not that they were all Jews
... not that they were all religious
... but that they – or most of them – were old.

The authority figures, Herod, Caesar and Quirinius were not young men. The shepherds were not children – not if it meant being out overnight. The *wise* men would have had to be old, otherwise in that culture they would not have been given the epithet. Joseph, legend has it, was old. He certainly seems to have departed this earth by the time Jesus is 30.

And as regards the book-ends, Simeon and Anna who see the child in the Temple are well up in years, while Elizabeth and Zacchariah are explicitly mentioned as being in their twilight years. Only Mary and Jesus can claim any youth.

The stories of Advent and Christmas are not about babies. Christmas is not – as we sometimes erroneously claim – a time for the kids.

ADVENT AND OLD PEOPLE

The stories of Advent and Christmas are about old people – the more so when we realise that the average life span for a man at the time when Jesus was born was around 34 years. The stories of Advent and Christmas are about old people whom God expects to prepare for and be changed by something very new.

It is not a babyfest. It is a celebration of God's investment in people whom others would claim to be 'past it'.

Some churches or voluntary organisations in certain housing areas may claim that no new initiatives can happen because there is 'an ageing congregation', or 'a high proportion of senior citizens'.

And a whole lot of middle-aged men ... (shall I say that again?) ... a whole lot of *middle-aged men* will defend inertia in the Church or society by saying that 'old folk couldn't cope' with this or that.

Let them say it! Let me say it! But don't let us defend our position by reference to anything to do with faith in the God and Father of our Lord Jesus Christ, who takes a positive delight in showing how those up in years can be the midwives of the new thing God wishes to do.

The story of Zacchariah and Elizabeth is a funny story. It's about an elderly minister, an old priest, who has done the religious thing year after year, and has probably grown pretty blasé about what God is like.

He has seen dozens of Passovers celebrated; he has seen and heard thousands of people pray for healing or for political deliverance; he might even have expounded the message of salvation himself. But he doesn't expect anything actually to happen.

So, when an angel greets him as he is looking after the incense altar, he wonders whether it is actually incense he is burning or whacky baccy. And when the angel tells him that he and his post-menopausal wife are going to be parents, he imagines that both of them must be affected by hallucinogenic substances.

But hadn't he read the Bible? Didn't he remember that every Jew claimed to be descended from Abraham who was 99 and from Sarah who was 90 when Isaac was conceived? And so, for forgetting his heritage and for doubting that God could do anything new with people who were old, Zacchariah is made dumb until Elizabeth produces the child who will be called John.

You can just imagine the consternation that would go round the village they came from, as it would circulate in any town where a minister used to talking suddenly could not speak, and his wife who was lifting her pension began to enquire about maternity benefit.

But this is the way it is with God. There is no retirement in the kingdom of heaven and there is no writing off the elderly as if they, who have to cope with changes in every facet of life, would find a change in their religious life impossible to deal with.

NEW LIFE AMONG THE OLD

Last year, I was working in Australia and shared in a gathering of people from churches in the Melbourne area.

I was intrigued by one woman's story. She was in her mid-70s. She was or had been a church organist. But she didn't want to talk about the good old days when they had a choir of thirty and the church was full. She wanted to talk about the excitement she felt at what was presently happening to her and to others in an economically depressed public housing area.

For years they had watched their old church building become emptier and more irrelevant to the people who lived nearby. The congregation was becoming more and more elderly.

They appointed a young woman to be their minister who assessed the situation with her people, and then proposed that they should stop worshipping in the church, and they should stop worshipping on a Sunday. Instead they would move into the community centre and worship on a mid-week evening. There, rather than gather as strangers, they would begin every Wednesday with a community meal.

So, the congregation – this elderly bunch – agreed that for the good and growth of the kingdom of God, they would sacrifice what they had been used to all their lives and do something different.

And this former organist in her mid–70s was just ecstatic about how they now had three times as many people at worship as before, how they now were linked into the community, how they now had children and young adults in their midst, how they now had changed the way they worshipped and sang to include rather than exclude strangers.

And as I looked at her, I realised that I wasn't looking at a 75-year-old organist, I realised I was looking at Sarah and Elizabeth and Anna – other old women to whom, in the Body of Christ, she is closely related. And these women – all of them – along with the men who stood by or obstructed them, are called to be midwives of the new order which God is about to initiate.

INITIATING THE NEW ORDER

This expectation of God that adults will embrace and initiate a new order, despite the odds seeming to be stacked against it, flows from the narrative of the birth of John the Baptist right through the ministry of John's cousin, Jesus.

There is a moment in Mark's Gospel when Jesus is predicting to Andrew, Peter, James and John that the world will not be a safe place, even though he has come as its saviour.

You will hear of wars and rumours of wars.
Nation will rise against nation, kingdom against kingdom,
There will be earthquakes in many places; there will be
famines.

... and before Jesus says any more, maybe we want to interject,

We know what you're talking about.

... because we – all of us, irrespective of our age – have been aware of nation rising against nation; and it has not been limited to the Second World War. It has been much more recent: in the Falklands, in the Gulf, in Israel–Palestine, in Indonesia, in Yugoslavia, in the Ukraine, in Afghanistan.

And you and I, irrespective of our age, have witnessed albeit via television pictures the ravages of earthquake and famine and flood – whether that be in Ethiopia or in Thailand or in Los Angeles, Worcester or York.

And with the possibility of a transatlantic co-operation in a new breed of Star Wars defence systems, we may be justified in wondering whether we are living in the end times. Whether, with the new political world order and the incessant ravages on the environment, humanity will be around for much longer.

Yet just as Zacchariah and Elizabeth, who thought that old age spelt slow-down, were confronted with pregnancy, so in Jesus' eyes what seems like the end times are identified by Jesus as unpremeditated labour pains.

These signs ... are the birth pangs of a new age.

For people of faith, pessimism is never an option, nor is apathy.

For people of faith, even those who feel keenly within themselves an anxiety about the way society is going or about the destiny of the world, the word of Jesus is the antidote to despair. It does not say that everything will be easy; it says that the hostility of nations or problems with the environment have to be seen as preparation for a new age, for new birth.

And the people of God are recruited to be midwives of the new order which God wishes to bring about in our societies, and in our world.

That, essentially, is what we are in the Church: not a collection of complainers who sing that things can only get worse, but an odd assortment of midwives who in the midst of confusion pray and believe and prepare for the new thing which God intends to happen.

4 The guardianship of creation

Texts: Jeremiah 5:20–25; Matthew 7:24–27

> *Your wrongdoing has upset nature's order, and your sins have kept away her bounty.*

There are some people in the Bible who are always associated with a particular attitude or circumstance:

Thomas is known for his doubting;
Martha for her obsession with housework;
Solomon for his wisdom;
Ruth for her loyalty;
Job for his unmerited suffering.

And then there's Jeremiah … whom some people would see as a dour Calvinist before his time, a cynical spectator on the life of the world, a forecaster of doom.

That's a bit unfair on Jeremiah.

For while his critique of the society in which he lived is not overwhelmingly favourable, he states clearly that his intention is not only to pull down but also to build up. He believes in a reconstructed nation.

But more than that, there is a concern in Jeremiah which one does not find in many other prophets. It is a concern that represents what is undoubtedly the greatest moral dilemma of our time, which threatens to become ever more serious as the century progresses.

Am I talking about the artificial prolongation of life? ... No. Am I referring to the issue of human sexuality? ... No. Am I talking about the possibility of genetically modifying embryos until you have the child of your choice in terms of IQ, hair colouring and other attributes? ... No.

I'm talking about the global environment and what we do with it – an issue on which the teaching and preaching of the Church, Protestant and Catholic, has been gloriously silent; an issue to which our hymnwriters, with the exception of those in the southern hemisphere, pay scant attention: 'All things bright and beautiful' and 'We plough the fields and scatter' are songs that celebrate the goodness of God in creation; they do not deal with our stewardship of the natural order.

This is an issue which reports of the Church rarely address. For while we have endless debates about the conservation of historic buildings, and the rights and wrongs of gambling, drinking, homosexuality or the lottery fund, we devote a derisory amount of effort to reflecting on how, under God, we treat the earth. And this despite the fact that the Bible begins and ends in a garden ... despite the fact that half, if not two thirds, of Jesus' parables refer to natural phenomena ... despite the fact that two of the most favourite psalms in all traditions – 'The Lord is my shepherd' (Ps.23) and 'I lift my eyes to the hills' (Ps.121) – are both rooted in a sense of God's presence, either indwelling or communicated through creation.

It is perhaps in the prophecy of Jeremiah that the relationship between humanity and nature as ordained by God is most concisely spelt out.

THE ECOLOGY OF JEREMIAH

It is in Jeremiah that we discover what was evident to the wandering Jews in the desert – that from time to time God calls on, speaks to, the earth, to be a witness for what he is doing and against what humanity has done:

Let the earth listen and be witness,
I am going to bring ruin on those
who have said all is well,
when all is not well (6:19 & 14)

It is in Jeremiah that we discover (though there is also plentiful evidence in the psalms) that God intended nature in its dependability and changeability to offer its maker a hymn of praise more mellifluous and diversely textured than any human composer could imagine or any choir could sing:

These are the words of the Lord
who gave the sun for a light by day and the moon
and the stars in their courses,
who cleft the sea and its waves roared. (31:35)

And it is in Jeremiah that we discover that God has made a direct correlation between the behaviour of humanity towards the earth and the security of the human race:

How long must the country lie parched,
and its green grass wither?
No birds and beasts are left
because its people are wicked,
because they say,
'God does not see what we are doing.' (12:4)

It is to this last aspect of Jeremiah's teaching that I want to attend.

His prophecy has hardly begun when he begins to identify a serious disruption in society. He points out that the failure to respect God as the Maker of the world, the bountiful giver of the created order, the failure to value the limits that God has put on the land and the sea, and the failure to be grateful for the fixed seasons of the year all contribute to a denial of respect for the earth and a senseless exploitation, which in turn leads to the earth's being unable to provide for humanity.

Your wrongdoing has upset nature's order
and your sins have kept away her bounty.

CONTEMPORARY WARNINGS

I am compelled to address this neglected issue, because all summer it has tormented me, as alarm bells have rung in place after place.

I met a retired mathematics professor, David Read from Dallas, Texas, who in his 70s gave up being a Democrat and became a Green and participated in the anti-globalisation protests in Seattle because even in his retirement he felt an urgency about the issue.

Two weeks later, I was at a conference where another retired professor, the church historian Adrian Hastings, passionately moved away from his text to stress that what we did with the environment was the most crucial issue of the new millennium, and he warned that time was short.

Shortly after this, I worked for ten days in Chicago where everyone drives their own individual car even though they are travelling alongside regular train routes, and where nobody seems worried that the USA is per capita the biggest polluter on earth. There I heard the since-substantiated rumour that George W. Bush (then Republican presidential candidate) said nothing about the environment because he was backed by Texan petrochemical industries. It's as crazy as having a government health ministry sponsored by Imperial Tobacco.

And then to Amsterdam, where not only do people increasingly use bikes, electric cars and trams, but where there is a national concern that the rising level of the North Sea might not be contained by the dikes.

All this was epitomised soon after in the UK, when unprecedented climatic conditions caused by global warming caused Worcester to resemble Venice, while the road transport lobby, surely cognisant of the fact that pollution has brought on the meteorological crisis, demanded that fuel become cheaper so that more people can exercise their freedom of choice to burn petrol.

And as a kind of counterpoint to this concern we have the recurrent theme of BSE and CJD, and what happens when, in order to fulfil the great British appetite for more meat, both the factory and natural farming of animals introduce into the food chain substances about which even a 12-year-old school child would be doubtful.

Your wrongdoing has upset nature's order
and your sins have kept away her bounty.

I want, on the basis of Jeremiah, to suggest some appropriate responses on the part of biblical people to the present parlous state of the relationship between humanity and nature.

THE THINGS OF THE EARTH AS GIFT, NOT RIGHT

The 20th century has witnessed an increasing devaluation of language and a resulting confusion between two very different entities.

If you go into a fast-food restaurant, for example, people will frequently say, 'I need a 12-ounce hamburger with fries and onions on the side and I need a chocolate milk shake.'

Now, when you look at the size of some of the diners, you very quickly realise that the last thing they *need* is giant hamburgers full of fat and milk shakes full of sugar. That may be what they want; it is not what they need.

In the same way, rights and privileges have become mixed up. People see the possession of a television, building their house where they want it, watering a garden with a hose pipe in an arid region as basic human rights.

No such thing was ever agreed by the United Nations or decreed by God. The right to education, clean drinking water and freedom to worship are paramount human rights. Everything else is just a luxury.

Nor are many of our expectations of the earth legitimate in the context of what is appropriate for the whole planet. We carelessly expect water for washing cars during spells of drought, or hamburgers that require the Guatemalan rainforest to be torn down for cattle grazing, or carnations and strawberries for British dinners in December that cause countries like Ethiopia and Mexico to devote their fertile land and limited water supplies to pandering to Western tastes. Such expectations in the real world have to be set against not just what is possible, but what is just for the earth and all its people.

But sadly that is something which the Northern nations cannot comprehend. And their lack of understanding becomes dangerous when we realise that it is the same Northern nations whose voices and opinions prevail simply because they control the international news media, the telecommunications industries and the worldwide web.

We live in a finite world. There is not enough oil to last for ever. So if we demand for our second and third cars as much petrol as we want, as cheaply as we can get it, what is the knock-on effect for developing nations who also deserve access to this natural mineral? Are they to be left out? And are our grandchildren going to have to visit a museum to see what oil and petrol look like because we, their grandparents, sacrificed its finite supplies on the altar of insatiable greed?

Those who see the earth as supplying their wants rather than as being a gift of God's grace, will forever get needs and privileges mixed up.

It is clear in the Bible that where selfishness becomes the accepted creed of a nation, God does not heed that nation's prayers, and nature fails to deliver her kindly gifts. No amount of genetic engineering will make finite resources supply infinite demands.

THE EARTH AS FRIEND, NOT ENEMY

This would seem to be a fairly easy matter to contemplate. However, the recent response of our political leaders to the effects of global warming has been full of fighting talk.

It is almost as if the imperialistic language of the past, which saw the red, yellow or black man as the savage enemy, needing to be tamed and taught a lesson, has been transferred to the earth.

We have to *fight* the encroachment of desert onto arable land,
we have to *defend* ourselves against the ravages of the sun,
we have to build *barricades* against rivers,
we have to *stockpile* against the lack of this, that or the other commodity.

Now, it may be that in the absence of a combative war, military rhetoric has to find employment elsewhere, but the demonisation of nature is not something which God encourages.

In the Gospels, whenever Jesus speaks of nature or draws examples from it, the images are never negative or demeaning of the natural order. When we are asked to look at the birds of the air, or to consider the lilies of the field, we are being asked by Jesus to draw ourselves into a relationship with nature similar to that which he obviously had. And it was not a relationship of adversaries, of enemies, of opposition.

If we admire something that has been wonderfully made, we cannot speak foul of it or misuse it. In the same way, we do not belittle those people whose conversation and gifts and skills we value. They are part of us and we are part of them. We stand in relationship to them and we will not demean them.

But it is those with whom we have no relationship and the arena of wonder we have never admired which we are more prone to disregarding and misusing.

When Jesus requests that we consider the birds of the air, the lilies of the field, we are being asked to befriend rather than demonise nature. And we are being asked to identify in the natural processes of the world a pattern of existence that is the antithesis to and the antidote for the frustration, stress and unhappiness which result from the insatiable desire to possess and to consume.

DISASTER AS PREVENTABLE, NOT INEVITABLE

One week in particular, I found the fatalism of the news reports highly disturbing. First the UK's Deputy Prime Minister, John Prescott, announced that extreme weather conditions were going to be the norm from now on. And later he foretold that the changes we would have to adapt to in the next fifty years included everything from the extinction of rare alpine plants to the disappearance of beaches in Spain and the Balearic Islands where Scottish holidaymakers love to sun themselves.

Now I do not doubt that scientific analysis and conjecture is accurate, but I question whether we should take this sitting down, as if there were no possibility that moral indignation and responsible living might begin to turn the tide.

There was a time in the '60s and '70s, when the CND movement was at its peak, that critics outside and cynics inside felt it could make little impact, because in the end it wasn't the protestors who had their hands on the button or who controlled the purse strings of the Ministry of Defence.

But the issue of the environment is not such a distant, objective, untouchable affair.

It is the amount of energy I choose to use,
it is the demand for unseasonal vegetables that I choose
to make,
it is the number of journeys by private transport that I
believe is my right,
it is the mountain of waste I decide not to recycle,
it is the investments in environmentally hostile firms I want
to profit from.
And for Christians, it is the distance I want to put between
the will of God and my lifestyle ...
All of this ultimately affects the state of the planet and the
consciences of those with whom I engage.

We are not victims of an environmental catastrophe over which we have no control. We are children of God called to be guardians of creation.

ROCK OR SAND?

Jesus once told a parable about the natural world. The parable was about two men who went to build a house – the one on solid rock, the other on sand. When the floods rose and the wind howled, the house on solid rock stood and the house on the sand collapsed.

But like all the parables of Jesus it was never meant to deal solely with its subject matter. Jesus was not giving a lecture on civil engineering or do-it-yourself house-building. He was pointing to an existential choice which is ours to make: to root ourselves on the solid rock of the word of God which sees the world as God's gift to be cherished, befriended and protected, or to root ourselves on the sand of endless selfish consumption, irrespective of the cost to the world or to our descendants.

What Jesus did was to offer a choice. What Jesus did not do was to make that choice for us.

5 In living memory

Texts: Joshua 4:1–8; Mark 9:1–8

MARKING THE MOMENT

There is something in the human condition which compels us to mark in different ways important moments in our lives.

It is insufficient just to remember that we met someone special, or saw something significant or did something surprising. We do not want such occurrences merely to be mental recollections. We want some more permanent means of registering that I met her, or was there, or did that.

Is it that we fear that others will not believe us and accuse us of making up stories? Is it because our memories might fail us and we need physical reminders? Or is it that when something important and unexpected happens to us, we feel it is like a gift, and we need to give something in return?

Let me be more specific, and detail two ways in which we mark important moments in our lives.

SOUVENIRS AND MEMENTOS

The first is that we might take away a souvenir.

If we go to the Van Gogh Museum in Amsterdam, we might like to take home one of the original paintings, but a lack of money and the presence of guards prevents us doing so. We settle instead for a copy, a print or a postcard of the painting that captured our attention. Or perhaps we visit the bulb fields near Alkmaar, and we are so impressed by the endless kilometres of tulips that we buy some bulbs to plant at home.

I remember preaching in Amsterdam one Sunday 25 years ago on the text:

'Remember Lot's wife.'

There was an American Southern Baptist in the congregation who was so impressed by the New English Bible translation of the scripture passage and by the fact that a preacher should think of expounding that particular text, that he bought a Bible as a souvenir of his visit and asked me if I would write something in it.

Not being prepared for this, I simply wrote the text, 'REMEMBER LOT'S WIFE' ... and signed it John L. Bell. Later I wondered what kind of domestic conversation might ensue when he returned home if his wife were not a believer but felt curious enough to read the inscription in the front of his new souvenir Bible.

Taking home a souvenir – or simply taking a photograph – may be one way in which we deal with our compulsion to respond to a special place, a special person, a special activity that has affected us.

A different response, but an equally natural one, is to leave something of ourselves in the location where the special meeting or incident happened.

We go, perhaps in our younger years, for a walk in the country with someone we love, someone with whom we want to spend the rest of our lives. We vow that love to each other and, as if to witness to it, we carve our initials on the bark of a tree and surround them with the shape of a heart.

We go into an ancient Catholic church – a cathedral or an abbey. We are affected by the sense of history, of prayer being made here for centuries – maybe even of the presence of God – and Protestants, even the most obdurate, even the doubly die-hard Calvinists, find themselves lighting a candle, or putting a donation in an offering box.

Or – as happens sometimes in my country, Scotland – we climb a mountain and take with us a stone from the bottom of the mountain, or from the river bed. We take it to the top, because we know there will be a 'cairn' there, a heap of stones marking the summit, and we add our stone to those that others have carried. It is a memento of our achievement in climbing the hill.

This is a universal phenomenon – marking special events, special meetings, special achievements, either by taking a souvenir or by leaving in the place a memento of our being there.

It is universal; it is as old, at least, as the Bible; and it is something God encourages.

AN ANCIENT PEDIGREE

For is that not precisely what happened when the children of Israel walked through water for a second time.

The first time was the crossing of the Red Sea under the leadership of Moses. The second time was the crossing of the

Jordan as they entered the promised land under Joshua. And here not only are souvenirs taken but a memorial is made – and this by express command of God.

God tells Joshua to get one person from every tribe to lift a boulder from the bed of the river – a souvenir of the crossing – but not to take it with them to their new home. No. The twelve stones have to be made into a cairn – a visible monument as a reminder of how God kept his vow to bring the Hebrews to the promised land.

And this cairn, this stone monument, is intended not simply as a reminder for the current generation but also for their descendants. God's intention was that, in years to come, families might walk past that pile of stones, and perhaps a young child would say to her mother and father, 'What are these stones doing here?' And then the parents would tell the child and anyone else who was listening that these stones were a monument to how God kept his vow to bring his people to the promised land.

If we were to flip through the pages of the Old Testament, we would see other monuments, other stones which God had ordained to remind people of the story of their nation – and of the great things God had done.

Stones like the one Jacob erected after he had been given a dream of angels climbing up and down a ladder at the town called Luz. So important was the event that when Jacob had erected the monument he changed the name of the place to Bethel which means 'House of God' (Genesis 28:29).

Or the great stone that Samuel erected at Mizpah after the Israelites had defeated the Philistines in battle, the stone that was raised up as a monument and given the name Ebenezer which means 'Stone of Help' (1 Samuel 7:12).

LOST MEMORY

For centuries, perhaps, these fine monuments, even these mementos of great happenings, of great deliveries, of solemn promises, hold fascination for one generation and perhaps the next. But there comes a time when children and strangers stop asking about the cairns, the monuments, the stones ... and so the stories become forgotten. The deliverances, the victories, the promises are remembered no more. Human beings have both the desire to mark momentous occasions and the potential to forget the significance of their memorials.

When people sit round the war memorial opposite the Dam Palace in Amsterdam and take photos and smoke dope, is it because the stones remind them that this was once an occupied city in which there was a pogrom against Jews and resisters? Or has the monument lost its power to tell the story and just become a tourist attraction?

On the 6th August, the anniversary of the dropping of the first nuclear bomb on Japan, will those who gather silently at the memorial in Hiroshima remember only the horror of Japanese atrocities during the war? Or will they also remember the horror humanity unveiled on the 6th August 1945, namely that it had the potential to dismember in a day the whole created order which God had taken millions of years to perfect?

When people gather in the ruins of the old Coventry Cathedral, will the stones speak of the desolation which not only Germany visited on Britain, but in a much greater way the allies visited on Cologne and Dresden and Frankfurt?

Or are the stones in Hiroshima and Coventry losing their power to tell the full story, and instead offering themselves as locations for photo opportunities.

It is interesting to consider how a more recent pile of stones – the Berlin Wall – has made its way in fragments into hundreds of thousands of offices and bedrooms, sometimes as a reminder of the cost and futility of the cold war, but in other cases more as a fashion accessory.

It is perhaps because memorials – even the best – even the most God-ordained, do not always fulfil their potential and purpose, that Jesus seems to distrust them.

THE TRANSFIGURATION

Long before 6th August was Hiroshima Day, the Church designated it to be the Feast of the Transfiguration.

On the mountain, with Peter, James and John, there is a moment of divine and unique clarity, when Jesus is seen in a new light – talking with Moses the lawgiver and with Elijah the prophet, two great figures in Jewish history representing the rational and the intuitive sides of faith; the law and the prophets.

And Peter – as befits him – gets it wrong. Had cameras existed at that time, he would have seen it as a photo opportunity. But there being no cameras, he wants to do the most appropriate thing – build shelters, one for each of the three heroes of the faith, perhaps the biggest for Jesus.

These would be lasting memorials of this supreme revelation. In later years he could bring his family and show them the precise spot where it happened, and the precise stones beneath which Moses and Elijah and Jesus sheltered.

But Jesus will have none of it.

He neither needs nor wants a sacred pile of stones which – among other things – would tie him and the Gospel to one nation, one country, one time in history. This is perfectly consistent with the rest of his life where he bequeaths to his disciples no property, no possessions, no diary, not even a grave.

He is the man without memorials, because he knows that memorials limit the memory to one place, and one culture, and that in time memorial stones lose their power to transmit importance. They fail to speak.

THE TANGIBLE REMEMBRANCE

Yet soon after, knowing that human beings do have a need for tangible signs of great things that have happened, Jesus does something which is startling in its simplicity and its universality.

He does something which is not tied to the geography of one land, or the history of one nation. He initiates and blesses a ceremony that can happen in any language, in any nation, at any time, as long as there are on earth human beings who hunger and thirst.

By blessing bread and breaking it,
by blessing wine and sharing it,

by naming these natural things as symbols of his love
which is willing to be broken and poured out for all ...
by initiating what we call the sacrament of Holy Communion,
Jesus ensures, for all time and for all people,
that not just the story of his life and death,
but also his power to forgive, to heal, to transform
is presented and made real
whenever his example and command are followed.

You can marvel at cairns, at memorials, at monuments, in Israel–Palestine, in Amsterdam, in Hiroshima, but inevitably you have to leave them.

But when you receive the bread and wine which are offered at communion, you discover and celebrate that Jesus Christ will never leave you.

6 The controversies of faith and failure

Texts: Job 38:1–18; John 6:41–45

> *We know his father and mother. How can he say, 'I have come down from heaven?'*

COOKING – THE BOOKS

In almost any bookshop you enter these days, there will be a large section which has grown immensely in the past ten years, devoted to cooking:
- French cooking
- Japanese cooking
- cooking with cream
- cooking with a microwave oven
- cooking while waiting for your hair to dry

... and when you look inside these books, the recipes and the pictures are often surrounded by words like SIMPLE –

'This simple recipe will only take half an hour.'

or words like SUCCESS –

'This simple recipe is a great success at any dinner party.'

What never happens is that the books show you what happens if the SIMPLE recipe turns out to be a DISASTER.

There are no pictures of the SIMPLE CHEESE SOUFFLÉ which comes out of the oven and flops over to one side like an old bashed hat.

There are no pictures of the faces of your guests when you bake them a SIMPLE VICTORIA SPONGE CAKE – only to discover that because you were cooking while waiting for your hair to dry, you thought that you had sprinkled the cake with icing sugar, but actually it was garlic salt.

No pictures of upset guests ...

But I suppose that books which try to enthuse you about their subject would never sell if they talked about the dangers.

Books about fishing do not have pictures of people who have leant too far out the boat and fallen in.

Books about playing the bagpipes do not say what you should do if the neighbours start to complain.

All of which makes the Bible a unique book.

Because, while the Bible is there to encourage people to believe in God,
- not every story is a success story;
- not every story is about people who started believing in God and discovered that overnight they had more money, more friends, a happier life;
- not every story says that Moses or Jeremiah or Jesus always got it right.

In fact, in the Bible, very few people get it right.

The Bible is not a cookery book with SIMPLE RECIPES and guaranteed RESULTS.

JOB IS HARDLY A SUCCESS STORY

The story of Job is neither a short story nor a success. It takes up 42 chapters and moves through both bane and blessing.

At the beginning of the book of Job, the story of this law-abiding, respectable family man who believes in God has hardly begun when disaster after disaster strikes him.

He loses his wife,
he loses his family,
he loses his animals,
he loses his house.

He believes in God and yet he becomes the victim of multiple disasters. (That doesn't say much for believing in God, does it?)

The next thirty or more chapters have to do with Job and some friends trying to work out what went wrong:

Why should bad things happen to good people?
How can God let this happen to a friend?
What secret thing must Job have done which brought
on this punishment.

And after thirty chapters of argument, there are no helpful conclusions, no resolutions. At the end, having failed to find the reason or remedy for his misery from his three friends, Job is given an interview with God.

We expect that God will now make things easier for him, that God will be understanding and comforting. That's the kind of thing that God should do!

Then the Lord spoke to Job out of the tempest:

Who is this?
Brace yourself! Stand up like a man.
I shall put questions to YOU and YOU must answer:

Where were you when I laid the earth's foundations?
Who set its corner stone in place?
Who supported the sea at its birth?
Which is the way to the home of light?

... on and on, question after question, for about half an hour, as if Job hasn't had a hard enough time already. (And this is supposed to encourage us to believe in God? Bring out the cookery books and let's try something easier!)

Yes, this is supposed to help us believe in God – for two reasons:

First, we are invited to recognise that faith does not claim to be an insurance policy against disaster. Anyone who thinks that if you believe in God you'll never have a hard time has never read the Bible.

Faith is not about avoiding failure, it's about what you believe and what you do when failure happens to you. And it is a cheap, cheating, bogus Gospel that says, 'Believe in God and everything will always be well.'

But second, the story of Job helps us to believe because it says that life is not logical. It is a mystery – or rather it is a sequence of mysteries. Job is wholly concerned with the mysteries of his own suffering. But the questions God asks Job – about how the world was made, how the sea was born, which is the way to the home of light – these and the hundred other questions point to the fact that we live in a world surrounded by the mystery of beauty, of imagination, of love.

And if we have never stopped to marvel at the mystery of creation which is above and before and around us, have we any right to think that the only mystery worth talking about is our own hard times?

What would you rather do: believe in a God who is surrounded by mystery and imagination and wonder, a God who allows us to experience failure as well as fulfilment? Or believe in a God who only deals with success stories?

NON-COOKERY-BOOK GOSPELS

It's not like a cookery book, the Bible, and this becomes even more evident when we get to the Gospels.

Most famous chefs who write cookery books, especially in Britain, also have their own television programmes: Delia Smith ... Keith Floyd ... Jamie Oliver.

Sometimes they go into other people's kitchens, or sometimes invite people into theirs. And the conversation is always very polite – parents talk about their children, wives talk about their husbands, film stars talk about their next movie.

There's never any argument or upset.

You never get someone saying to Delia Smith, 'I think you're a fraud and all your soups taste like bath water.'

You never get someone saying to Jamie Oliver, 'Why don't you give up cooking and try ballet dancing as a career?'

Oh no, celebrities are treated like celebrities. It wouldn't sell books or interest people in the product to have the star of the show ridiculed in public.

But when we come to the Bible, which is supposed to encourage belief, and to the Gospels, where the principal figure is Jesus, the Son of God, what do we get?

- a record of complete obedience and respect wherever he went?
- stories of how everyone agreed with everything he said?
- the support and encouragement of all who heard him?

Not a bit of it!

We know his mother and father!
How can HE say 'I have come down from heaven?'

What we read in John's Gospel about the reaction to Jesus from his own fellow citizens is typical of what appears again and again in the Gospels. Indeed, I would reckon that almost a third of the story of Jesus has to do with opposition to him and failure.

There can be no major figure in the history of the world religions about whom so much opposition and disbelief is recorded in the story of his life.

And does this help us to believe?

I would say yes – definitely.

It is precisely because within human history and in human language Jesus so often contradicts what we expect God to be like, that in the end we discover that we are not dealing with someone who simply makes us feel comfortable, but with a God who wants us to change.

If, for you, believing in God depends on God's agreeing with all you think is important, you are looking for a God who is slightly smaller than your ego. But if you are prepared to engage with Jesus Christ who is both controversial and no one's fool, then you are in touch with the God who never lets us stay the same.

It intrigues me that the longer I look at Christ, the more my understanding of him and of God's expectation of my life changes.

I used to think that because Jesus had twelve male disciples, Christianity was really a man's world, until I realised that there are as many women disciples indicated in the Gospels as men, and that women – the Canaanite woman, Mary of Magdala – were the first evangelists, long before the church even got round to thinking about ordaining men.

I used to think – because I was fascinated by liberation theology – that Jesus was exclusively the saviour of the poor, until I noticed that in people like Matthew, and Joseph of Arimathea, and Nicodemus and Joanna and Susanna, and Simon the Pharisee, he was also a friend of the rich.

I used to think that Jesus was the Lord and Guardian of the Church, until I realised that on every occasion in the Gospels when he is within religious precincts he upsets people and is confronted with fierce opposition.

I used to think that Jesus knew it all – until I realised how many of his stories depended on listening to the experience of women in the kitchen, and men in the field, so that he could talk to other women in their kitchens and men in their fields.

I used to think that Jesus was impassive, cool, always in

control – until I realised that when his friend died, he not only wept openly but was deeply angry that such a thing should have happened.

I used to think that Jesus left a great legacy – until I realised that he left no books, no mementos, no possessions; that his only legacy – that his risky, fallible, flawed and unreliable legacy which he even still trusts – is you and I, his body in the world.

You will find few giant figures in the history of the world's religions who are derided from birth by critics because their family pedigree isn't exactly the stuff of which saviours are made.

You will find few giant figures in the history of the world's religions whose every utterance is a source of controversy and upset to those who should have been on their side.

Yet this is true of Jesus. And you are left concluding that either this is the Messiah, the son of the living God present in history, or that humanity has been hopelessly duped by a fraudster with no credentials.

The Bible does not invite us to accept passively a series of ancient facts. It invites us to enter into the adventure of believing, because from start to finish, through Job and Jesus, it is made plain that whatever we believe about God, God believes in us.

7 Looking for a new heaven and a new earth

Readings: Revelation 21:1–5a; Luke 19:1–10

ROME AD 80–100

The scene is Italy – Rome, in fact, and an estate on the banks of the Tiber.

And in the manor house there's a party going on – a lively party, a society party. It started before dusk and now the night has darkened outside. But it is still warm. It is a balmy evening.

The party has already spilled out on to the terracing, with people going back into the house to refill their glasses. But as we look we see a distinct movement away from the house as people pour out following the host.

He is giggling in a rather high-pitched voice, pleased by some novelty which only he knows about. He leads the crowd to the gardens that sweep down to the river.

And as he enters the gardens he begins to shout:

I'm going to light up the night.

And behind him the crowd take up his words and begin to chant in encouragement:

Light up the night!
Light up the night!

From somewhere or other a burning stick is passed to the host and he takes it to what looks like a heap of tree branches which jut up into the air. There is another shout, a frightened shout, as someone screams:

No!

But the voice is drowned out by the clamour of the others ... and in no time the branches are set alight and the bonfire blazes and, as the night around it lightens, we are able to make out that in the middle of the bonfire, tied to a pole, is a human being, a man. He is the one who shouted 'No'. He is the one who is about to be burned to death.

But no one hears his cry, for hardly has his funeral pyre been lit than the host has moved to another corner of the garden and to another bonfire-in-waiting, while all the while his guests chant relentlessly:

Light up the night!
Light up the night!

At the end of the first century, in Rome, the early Christian church was being severely persecuted by emperors like Nero and Domitian. Around this time, John of Patmos, the writer of the Book of Revelation, aware of the persecution befalling the church, was given a series of visions, which culminated in his writing the words:

I saw a new heaven and a new earth.

ANALYSIS PARALYSIS

But it wasn't the Book of Revelation I was reading the other week. It was a book I saw in a shop in New Mexico. When I first saw it, I thought the title was *Feed your piranha.*

So I lifted it up to see how many fingers or toes you offered to this exotic pet per day – only to discover that the book was not called *Feed your piranha* but *Feed your paranoia.*

This equally intriguing title found me quickly opening the pages to discover all the things that could go wrong, even though one lived in a relatively stable Western democracy.

It gave statistics regarding one's chances of being struck by lightning, run over by a steam roller, hit by a rogue golf ball, and indeed eaten by a piranha. It indicated the likelihood of men my age developing prostate cancer, having a lobotomy and losing their memory (I forget what page that was on). It gave graphs about the chances of being afflicted by food poisoning, civil war or mistaking a bottle of turpentine for a bottle of gin. By the end of the book I was stunned to discover that I was still alive – though I suppose the odds in favour of dying while reading the book couldn't be calculated prior to publication.

In its very unique and tongue-in-cheek way, the book is a product of our times. For our times – our *Sunday Times*, our *New York Times*, our contemporary times – preserve a fascination for identifying what is wrong, and analysing the causes and symptoms without necessarily indicating the cures. And you, like me, might devour such information – especially when at the heart of this information is a reality which is palpably unjust.

I find it galling to read, as I did two weeks ago, that British company executives are the highest paid in Europe, earning on average £100,000 more than continental counterparts. And yet, though the top bracket earn over half a million pounds per annum before bonuses, workers' wages are significantly lower than those of their Japanese or German counterparts.

I find it absurd that George Bush should refuse to sign the Kyoto Accord on the grounds that developing nations are not being required to cut emissions – and this despite the fact that America with 7% of the world's population accounts for 25% of global warming; and despite the fact that the average American citizen is responsible for three hundred times the carbon monoxide emission of the average Mozambiquan.

I find it incredible that the Scottish salmon farming industry causes twice the amount of sewage to be discharged into the sea than the human population of Scotland but feels no responsibility for the pollution of inshore waters which is currently rendering some native shellfish lethal to eat.

I reeled with anger last week listening to a church minister, who is one of four in a new town of over 40,000 people, speak of how in the neighbouring, more historic town there are five ministers for a population of 15,000 people.

Such statistics, such figures, such indices of ignorance or of iniquity cause us to feel anger, disquiet or frustration … don't they? We wonder what is happening to our world. We wonder whether we can take in any more.

We become victims of that contemporary disorder which

George MacLeod, the founder of the Iona Community, called 'analysis paralysis'. And what can we do?

If we get passionately concerned, we might end up exhibiting pathological angst. If we feel threatened, we might become paranoid. If it is all too much for us, we might just set the television to show non-stop soaps or comedies to prevent ourselves from dealing with reality.

LOOK FOR A NEW HEAVEN AND A NEW EARTH

But if we believe in God, we look for a new heaven and a new earth. Because this is what John the Divine, John of Patmos, did when the statistics of murders, burnings, persecutions were getting grimmer by the day. And he did this not for a moment to escape wishfully from the conflagration and persecution around him, but because he expected that God, who loved the world, would act, would give an indication of a different reality that must happen, because God has not left the world to be damned.

Such a dream or vision or insight has always been the way in which God communicates with those whose ears and eyes are open and who expect God to defy logic because faith and time and the world are all mysteries.

In the past Isaiah and Jeremiah and Micah were the bearers of the forward-looking vision when the reality of the current times and the words of the religious and political commentators were barren. So, to a distressed and dispossessed people, words are spoken about how one day:

The lion will lie down with the lamb
and the young child will place its hand in the snake's den

... quite illogical. But such words were never meant to be logical. They were meant to enable dispirited people to catch a glimpse of God's intentions for this world and its history.

Again and again, in words but often in actions, God reveals an alternative reality, an indication that dire and depressing though circumstances may be, to those who are sensitive, who feel the pain, there is also granted the possibility of an alternative scenario and a new heaven and a new earth, starting here.

ZACCHEUS

Was that not just exactly what happened when Jesus walked into Zaccheus' house and had a meal?

Had people not calculated how much he had swindled from them because of over-zealous taxation and money-lending malpractice? Had people not mumbled about how few guests ever went into his house? Had people not estimated how long his tyrannical hold over the tax system would continue? Had they not calculated and looked forward to the retirement date of this social parasite?

Then into this suspected, analysed, proscribed life of a reprobate comes Jesus Christ looking for his dinner. And because this man is shown *not* a vision of his imperfection, *not* a graph table of how much he had swindled, but converting love and hospitality, he is changed. And the upshot is that everyone else, particularly his debtors, benefits from his transformation.

It is not by the calculation of odds nor by the tabulation of sinister statistics that the world is moved forward; it is by a vision of an alternative reality.

And because in the past it was given to the prophets to provide the vision, and because supremely in Jesus such glimpses into reality were offered, it must still happen here – if this is indeed the Body of Christ.

For God has not given up on the world, and the church and its worship must be where a new heaven and a new earth can be glimpsed.

SIGHTINGS

I believe this personally because I have seen it here in Iona Abbey

I remember fifteen years ago, when Mandela was still in prison, and the news of South Africa grew grimmer by the day, as a fortress mentality developed there, and as people here felt impotent to do anything and maybe did not care too much anyway.

I remember here in this Abbey, on the last evening of the week when people gathered to celebrate communion round a table, two young men joined hands high in the air and sang *Nkosi Sikel' iAfrica* ... God Bless Africa. One was white and British – representing the nation which in South Africa introduced concentration camps to the world – and the other was black and a Xhosa whose schooling had been disrupted by township violence and whose presence in Scotland was monitored by the South African police.

And suddenly, in that action – of joining hands and singing – there was a glimpse of a new heaven and a new earth, a possibility that things could change and all would be different and that our deep prayers and our demonstrations would not be in vain. God raised up that sign.

And I remember last year, the Jubilee year, my colleagues and I were responsible for producing a liturgy, an act of worship to celebrate the biblical requirement that debts be cancelled and people burdened with debt be restored to their full dignity. I remember something which happened on Iona and in York Minster and in a Lutheran cathedral in Karlskroner, Sweden, and in a Catholic church in New Orleans.

The liturgy allowed people, if they wished, to make signs of their commitment to God's future of justice and responsible living. Towards the end of the service, people could engage in any of four symbolic actions. One of these required worshippers to come up to the altar on which there was a basket with small pieces of string, each tightly knotted. They were invited to take a piece of string and remember someone who was indebted to them morally or financially, someone they had not forgiven, someone who was the victim of their unwillingness to let the past be put behind them. Then, in front of the cross of Jesus, they could untie the knot and lay the string on the altar and declare before God their decision to cancel the debt, to forgive.

And I watched grown men cry and teenagers cry and proud people come away changed, because in that action they glimpsed a new heaven and a new earth where reconciliation might win the day rather than hatred.

This must be what the church and liturgy are about.

For certainly in the early church, when the present was hostile and the future seemed uncertain, it was John the Divine's envisioning of God's alternative reality which inspired hope and nourished faith when it was most despondent.

If we are here either to replay an outdated tradition which no one understands or to sample liturgical fruits from different places and choose which one suits our palate, then let us admit we are fetishists, for this is not the sighting of an alternative reality.

THE EUCHARIST

Jesus, knowing that his time to leave the earth had come, did not preach a sermon or offer a mantra for constant repetition. He took bread and wine. And in this bread and wine he offered a vision of a new heaven and a new earth.

For in this sacrament it is revealed for those whose eyes are open that life is about sharing, not about hoarding ...

And in this sacrament it is revealed for those whose eyes are open that life is about being broken, not about remaining inviolable ...

And in this sacrament it is revealed that the things of this earth –
> not just the people of this earth,
> not the souls on this earth,
> not even the religions of this earth,
but the products of this earth, as natural as bread and wine, are the means by which God makes heaven known here.

We cannot take this bread and wine with open eyes and remain self-obsessed; we cannot eat this bread and drink this wine and remain detached; we cannot eat this bread and drink this wine and treat the earth as if it were a disposable rag on which we wipe ourselves.

For here is a new heaven and a new earth meant for now,
    meant for you
    with love
    from God.

8 Not peace, but a sword

Texts: 1 Kings 3:16–28
       Matthew 10:32–39

THE CRYING GAME

If you have never seen the film *The Crying Game*, then permit me to spoil for you one of its most memorable moments.

The film is – among other things – about the relationship between an IRA terrorist-with-a-conscience and a hairdresser he meets while on a mission to undermine the government in London. He sees her through the hairdresser's shop window, and later develops a relationship by becoming one of her customers. She is of Asian extraction and is the perfect foil to his brusque, unsophisticated Celtic manner. You feel – as a viewer – that she is the means of his redemption as an individual if not as a terrorist.

In the course of their relationship, intimacy develops, though she is hesitant to be bedded on the first occasion that might be possible. But in a subsequent encounter, the camera offers the view of the terrorist as he gently and lovingly undresses his girlfriend. By page three standards she is not very stunning, for she is a slightly built creature. However, as he moves down to her nether regions the audience – who have become the terrorist undressing his beloved – gasp to discover that she is kitted out with a penis. She is not female at all but a transvestite, and he and we have been oblivious to this possibility.

Were it to happen in real life, one can imagine the agonising incredulity as what appeared to be one reality was suddenly revealed to be quite the opposite. It's the kind of moment in which personal history and future prospects are all up for reinterpretation. The mind does somersaults trying to make sense of what has been and what now is to come.

Is it a moment reserved only for fiction? Certainly not.

A MALIGN SURPRISE

It is the kind of moment which was visited on the personnel manager of an engineering firm in an Ayrshire town, in the mid-1970s. It was the era when indigenous industry was being bought up by multinational corporations. Often large local businesses employing a substantial proportion of the town's labour force, the majority were bought over by national or international predators.

Economic rationalism being one of the in-vogue practices, it was not long before the patents that had been purchased were transferred elsewhere and more lucrative production plants in England, France, North America or Taiwan produced what had once been the town's originals.

The personnel manager was asked to make a list of over a hundred men who could be deemed surplus to requirements. It was a gruelling task because he had to identify men he knew and trusted, who had gone through the firm with him, who were his friends – as well as newcomers with no long-term loyalty. When he presented the list to his superior, he was told to add his name at the bottom.

How would he feel?

How would he feel as thirty years of devoted service to a local industry were pulverised? What did this say about the value of his work, about the integrity of the new owners? And what did it mean for his future – and for that of his family in a town where the dole-queues were lengthening each day with middle-aged men doomed, it seemed, to perpetual redundancy?

It's the kind of moment when all that has been and all that is to come suddenly needs to be reinterpreted.

A HOLY SHOCK

If we can, in any way, empathise with the fictional IRA soldier or with the real personnel manager in Ayrshire, we may be able to share the shock of Jesus' first disciples when they heard him say the words:

I did not come to bring peace ... but a sword.

Suddenly and without warning all that they have presumed to be true about him, all that they have identified as winsome and contradictory in his teaching is turned on its head – and he begins to sound like a terrorist.

What has happened to the one who embodied reconciliation, who preached not just love of the neighbour, but love of the enemy? What has happened to the one who was presumed to value families, as in further utterances he indicates that his purpose is to come between father and son, mother and daughter – and this despite his encouragement of others to honour their parents? What has happened to the one who, in his consorting with foreign women, in his embracing of diseased people, in his invitation of outsiders into closed-session banquets, indicated that he had come to end division not to instate it?

Why does Jesus say this?

There are a number of possibilities ...

THE DIVINE PREROGATIVE

One is that he was using the divine prerogative. What divine prerogative?

I refer to the habit God reveals in dealing with the children of Israel whereby when they think they have God 'sussed', when they think that they know exactly the mind of God or can envisage the personality of God, God forces them into a double-take.

They think that God is a male warrior, then God reveals that he or she is in fact a midwife.

They imagine God as being steely and dispassionate, and discover tears on God's cheek.

They depict God as eternally passive, then Jacob, limping, witnesses to God's penchant for wrestling.

And, as such diverse figures as Abraham and Jonah discover, the inscrutable mind of God sometimes changes when compassion or divine whim determine that the presumed judgement, the advertised punishment, will not in fact be fulfilled.

Maybe Jesus was exercising the divine prerogative.

THE HARD MAN

Or maybe Jesus was refusing to allow himself to be seen as a soft touch.

For I imagine that then, as now, there would be devotees and admirers keen to domesticate Christ and make him the lap-dog of religion rather than God's *agent provocateur*.

In some parts of the country and the world where I work, I am constantly aware of how the radical, transforming, cutting-edge Gospel of Jesus is transubstantiated into hedonistic pap, as new consumer-friendly churches and some older traditions try to make Christianity as soothing and succulent as possible. The Gospel, castrated of its seminal power, becomes a mere balm. One goes to church not to be confronted with the awesome mystery and amazing grace of God, but to get what makes you feel good – as if the Maker of all things could be reduced to a saccharine spoonful of spineless piety.

Then, as now, there would be people desperately keen to ensure that Jesus was a meek and gentle guru. And maybe he just blew a fuse – which would not be irregular. Jesus does get angry, even if few sermons and fewer hymns mention his righteous indignation.

I did not come to bring peace but a sword.

Maybe he said it because he was exercising the divine prerogative ... maybe he said it to indicate that he was not a soft touch.

THE GOSPEL TRUTH

Or maybe he said it because it is true.

For the purpose of God in history, as I see it, is not to ensure that the prejudices as well as the wisdom of one generation transfer without question to the next. The purpose of God in history is to challenge and convert what have been malpractices, defective ideologies and fond though misguided assumptions about the world and its people and its Creator. And if this means that there is a breach required between father and son, mother and daughter, then God reserves the sole right to let that happen.

God does not countenance a marriage being dissolved because of the predatory behaviour of a third party. God does not remain indifferent when the state or the advertising industry drives a wedge between parent and child. While it is difficult from scripture to validate the kind of Victorian family values which many of us are presumed to espouse, it is clear that God meant covenanted relationships and familial relationships to be respected.

But God also reserves the right where one generation has got it wrong to prevent the deficiencies or the prejudices or the misinformation of that generation from being transferred to the next.

Two months ago, when I was in Nepal, I met a man who knows this intimately. His name is Chitra. He is a university graduate in economics who was in a respected position in the Communist party and had a civil service post. He became a Christian through attending the funeral of a distant relative, and from that day on, all things changed.

The sword was swung: his grandmother forbade him to enter her house, his predominantly Hindu village ignored him, his father disinherited him and told the police he was an enemy of the state, the Communist party threatened to kill him. And all this happened because he had done nothing other than to declare his love for God and his love for them even in the face of their rejection.

Sometimes I wish that the same sword would swing again, though not perhaps in as menacing a fashion as it did within the household of Chitra. For I am convinced that in this new century there are practices and presumptions espoused by my generation which are contrary to the revealed will of God, but yet are never on the agenda of many Christian people.

For almost two months on either side of New Year, I was working in four continents, and everywhere I went people were lamenting the vagaries of the weather. Now, as a Scot, I should have found this perfectly acceptable. But it was indeed exceptional.

In the Upper Clarence region of New South Wales, farmers were selling off their cattle or their land because of a nine-year drought, which was exacerbated by the battering of the land just after new year by hailstones the size of a fist which did twenty million dollars' worth of damage in two hours.

In Auckland, New Zealand, where it was cloudy and rained on New Year's Day, I met an inhabitant who said that the season used to be the best of the year, but in the past decade sun and fine weather have no longer been guaranteed during the holiday season.

In Waterloo, Ontario, two weeks later, people were reporting a snowfall more severe than anything known in the last forty years.

Meanwhile much of England was drying out from irregular dousing, while in the Netherlands people feared what would happen should the polar ice cap continue to melt and the sea level around the 'low countries' continue to rise.

Of course we know what it is and we know the cause. But is the next generation – or indeed this one – going to continue with the wisdom of its progenitors who believed that you can do what you like to the earth and still survive.

I hope that in the Christian Unions of university colleges which produce the future captains of British industry, there will be some discerning people who will read again John's Gospel and stumble over the realisation that the incarnation did not happen because God loved humanity. I do not read anywhere in John's Gospel that God so loved privatised religion that he became incarnate; I read that God so loved the *world*. I do not read in the Letter to the Colossians that all souls or all religious people are connected through Christ; I read that *all things* – the world, its creatures, the cosmos, the powers and principalities – *all things* cohere in Christ.

We need in this day and age a radical appraisal of that creeping dualism which separates the concerns of Christian faith into legitimate and illegitimate categories. No, we don't need an appraisal, we need Christ to come with a sword and hack to bits this false but comfortable divide!

I hope that students of scripture, lay and professional, will discern in the Psalms, in Jeremiah, in Isaiah, in the teaching of Jesus, in the Revelation of St John, the Gospel injunction to care for the earth rather than to abuse it. I hope that these same people will create havoc in their households and their classrooms and the boardrooms they may one day enter, so that in the avaricious privileged world there may be heard voices of conviction and commitment challenging our presumptions that we should go for endless growth despite the empirical fact that that road destines others to endless poverty.

Christ did not come here to bring peace but a sword – when the future of the world is at stake.

And I hope that in this nation, as elsewhere, there will be people of the generations after mine who will not be afraid to indicate to the church that in its quest for self-preservation and the iconisation of the past, it has sold short the Gospel.

I hope there will be young people in our churches who, not out of cant or faddishness, but out of love for God and the people of God, will not be afraid to say to their parents' generation as regards Christian witness or church practice: 'You got it wrong.'

For the word and person of Jesus are a sword intended to cut through the lies with which we comfort ourselves and to reveal the truth we avoid at our peril.

THE SWORD AND SOLOMON

And this essential separation of pretence from honesty and iniquity from justice is something which is at the root of that rather irregular story in the book of Kings in which Solomon shows the wisdom for which he is famed.

He is confronted with two female prostitutes, each of whom has recently given birth to a male child. The one mother smothered her child while she slept, the other mother had no such mishap. But both women lay claim to the living child and maintain that the dead child belongs to the other.

So Solomon calls for a sword and suggests that the living child be cut in two in order that both women get a half. One woman agrees with the verdict, the other pleads for the child's life and says that it should be given to her adversary. Then Solomon awards the baby to the one who was willing to surrender her claim in order to save the child's life. For clearly she was acting selflessly, out of love, while the other was acting selfishly, out of wickedness.

The sword in Solomon's hands was there to determine how much each woman loved.

The sword in Jesus' hands has exactly the same intention. For on the day when we answer to God for how we have conducted our lives, the definitive question will not be about our theological orthodoxy or our squeaky-clean character reference. It will be 'How much did you love? How much ...? How much did you really love?'

9 The umpteenth September 11th

Right at the start, I want to make it clear that the issue we are dealing with is far beyond the scope of a short chapter to encompass.

There are therefore a number of important issues I shall not be addressing:

the loss of innocent lives,

the heroism of fire-fighters

the war in Afghanistan

the projected war against Iraq

By declining to deal with them, I am not seeking for a moment to undermine their significance, but simply to allow myself to home in on one particular area of interest. Therefore I intend to:

a) Set a global and regional perspective in which to look at September 11th.

b) Make some comment on the response of the USA to the events.

c) Offer a biblical critique.

And I want to do this as objectively as possible.

Whereas on other issues of spirituality or lifestyle or biblical interpretation, I have frequent recourse to anecdote, personal or otherwise, this will be minimised here. The matter is too large to be looked at through the subjective lens of one person's mind or experience.

~~But I nevertheless begin by stating the personal reasons for~~
my interest in this issue.

PERSONAL INTEREST

I spend up to three months a year in North America, most of that in the USA. On September 11th 2001, I was boarding a flight from Glasgow to London at the beginning of a trip to Australia via San Francisco. Literally the minute before I walked onto the plane, the television screen at the gate showed the second aircraft crashing into the World Trade Centre.

In the ensuing year, I have visited the USA four times and have travelled to San Francisco, Chicago, New York, Indianapolis, Orlando and Rochester, among other venues. I have talked – where possible – with people of different ages and backgrounds about their reaction. I say 'where possible' because not everyone wants to speak, nor, even if they do, are they necessarily able to articulate much except gut feeling. Three examples in chronological order may illustrate this:

a) December 2001, the first Sunday in Advent in a conservative Episcopal (Anglican) Church in Orlando. The lectionary texts are about the 'end times'. It is impossible to avoid mentioning September 11th, but I do so cautiously, asking no more than whether this was the ultimate showdown that Jesus foretold. Afterwards I am amazed at the number of people who thank me for offering a biblical perspective. Until then September 11th had never been mentioned in preaching, but instead a patriotic hymn had been sung every Sunday.

b) February 2002, in the Middle Collegiate Reformed Church

in Manhattan. After morning worship, I am taken to lunch by people in the congregation. I sit beside a highly intelligent GP who asks what I think about September 11th and its aftermath. When I make a mild criticism of the US government policy, he – a Democrat – suddenly blurts out, 'Well, if it wasn't for the US, you'd never have got out of the Second World War.'

c) July 2002 in Rochester, New York, at a conference of Roman Catholic Musicians. I am teaching a four-seminar course on congregational song. I leave the last session open to deal with issues that are in people's minds and one woman speaking on behalf of a group of others asks, 'Could you give us some idea of what we do in church on this September 11th?'

SEPTEMBER 11TH

September 11th is also known as 9-11, for a peculiarly American reason. Whereas Britons dial 999, citizens of the USA dial 911 for emergency services. And on that day – among other things – the USA lost its virginity by rape. Or did it join the real world?

For in the real world, in all other continents, attacks on sovereign territory, even on democratically governed nations, have been occurring from the dawn of human history. And the USA almost singularly – since the American War of Independence – has *not* been the object of such predatory incursions.

But other nations have.

And what is embedded in the US psyche, if not the global conscience, as a day as memorable as 25th December, is but the latest of a procession of similar unwanted and unexpected violations of a nation's borders and security.

We could go back to 12th October 1492 when Columbus landed in the Bahamas and thus began a four-hundred-year assault on the sovereign territories of native Americans ...

Or we could go to 25th June 1497 when John Cabot set foot nearer New York on Newfoundland beginning that gradual process of claiming for Europe lands that belonged to nomadic tribes.

Or shall we go to the 18th January 1788 – a day which Aboriginal Australians remember with shame and regret. For that is when the first convicts exported from Britain began the first colony at Botany Bay.

Or what about the indeterminate day – from the British perspective – in 1833 when Britain invaded the Falklands ... or the 2nd April 1982 when Argentina tried to recapture its islands?

Or shall we note, in the last century, 10th May 1940 – a date remembered in Holland, Belgium and Luxembourg as the day when the five-year occupation of their territories was begun by Germany?

Or consider 20th August 1968, when Russian tanks rolled into Wenceslas Square in Prague.

Or – if you are a Republican in Northern Ireland – what about 4th August 1969, when British troops took over the 'security' of Ulster?

Or dare we remember 11th September 1973, when the USA

helped to overthrow and ultimately assassinate Salvador Allende, the democratically elected president of Chile?

There has been a procession of September 11ths from the dawn of history. It is not to belittle the USA experience, but it is to put it in a global context that I suggest that the prolonged attacks on and invasion of sovereign territories in Asia, Africa, Europe, the Pacific, South America are no less important to the psyches of these nations and no less important in the eyes of God than what happened to the USA on one day in 2001.

THE AMERICAS IN PERSPECTIVE

But there is another perspective that has to be noted which is specifically to do with the region surrounding the USA. In the immediate wake of September 11th, President Bush initiated his global war against terrorism. This was a both understandable yet rather hypocritical response if one sets against that intention the fact that for many decades the USA has been encouraging terrorism in or against the majority of its near neighbouring countries in Latin America.

Shall we recall that in 1898 the USA invaded the sovereign territory of Puerto Rico, and that in 1900, by the imposition of the Foraker Act, the US president acquired the right to appoint the governor, the cabinet and all the judges of that land? Yet on Dec 2nd 1901 the US Supreme Court decided that despite this occupation and overthrow, Puerto Ricans could not be considered as American citizens – a negative status which still pertains to the present day.

Or shall we recall that on Feb 12th 1901, the USA, which

had invaded the independent country of Cuba two years earlier, introduced the Platt Amendment which meant that virtually all of Cuba's domestic and foreign policies were determined or vetoed in Washington?

Or shall we recall that on July 3rd 1915, the USA invaded the sovereign territory of Haiti, enabled foreigners to purchase and own its lands and began a period in which historians have noted 'the Haitian population found itself subject to harsh racism'?

Or shall we come nearer our own time and consider – though not in detail – a military training establishment called, until January, 'The School of the Americas'? It is now called the Western Hemisphere Institute for Security Co-operation (WHSC). Under either title it has been operating in Fort Benning, Georgia, for 55 years. Since 1946 it has trained 60,000 Latin American soldiers and policemen who have been responsible for over 200,000 civilian deaths in Colombia, Guatemala and a host of other 'sovereign nations'. It has helped to overthrow or destabilise governments wherever in Central America nations threatened American security – and this under Democratic as well as Republican presidencies.

Thus in December 1981, after President Reagan had voted an extra 25 million dollars to keep in place the El Salvadorean government which Oscar Romero had vigorously opposed, the US-trained Atlacatl army battalion massacred 794 men, women and children in the Salvadorean village of El Mozote.

Some of us may remember in the 1980s watching a video of how in the Reagan era offerings were taken in Christian fundamentalist congregations in the Deep South to aid the contras in Nicaragua against the democratically elected government led by Daniel Ortega. Whatever money they raised would be small change compared to the hundred million dollars voted by the US congress in June 1986 to support the forces opposed to the elected government.

THE NON-STATE

I did not mention these things to the doctor in Manhattan who wanted to remind me that Europe should be eternally grateful to the US for baling it out of the Second World War. But I did bring up one subject which deeply offended him. I mentioned that September 11th was not the first time that the territory now known as the USA had been invaded.

'No indeed,' he replied, 'there was Pearl Harbor – December 7th 1941, when the Japanese assaulted sovereign US territory.'

And then I reminded him of a part of his nation's history of which he was not aware and of which I would not have been aware had I never visited Hawaii, but had continued to view it through Hollywood-tinted spectacles.

Hawaii used to be an independent Pacific nation – indeed a separate kingdom. If you go there you will see that Hawaiians are a different shape from most mainland US citizens, and the language is nothing like English or Spanish. Most words end in open vowels. It is a Polynesian language.

The people are extremely peaceable, so much so that on July 4th (note the date, July 4th) 1898 there was – as ever – no army. That was the day on which the descendants of Caucasian USA missionaries imprisoned Queen Liliuokalani,

~~disabled the police force and declared~~ – without consulting the Hawaiian people – that their kingdom was now a republic.

The fruit of their labours was completed on 12th August 1898 when sovereignty of Hawaii was transferred to the USA. It became a State without the consent of its majority Hawaiian population. The illegality of this act is admitted in a US Department of Justice Memo from 1988 which notes, among other things:

> *The Hawaiian Islands were foreign soil in 1898, some 2,100 miles beyond US territory. Based on the international law principle of extraterritoriality, a US joint resolution to annex Hawaii could not legally extend that far.*

And the memo goes so far as to quote how, during the annexation debates, a Congressman called Ball stated that any attempt at annexation would be 'to do unlawfully that which cannot be done lawfully'.

When I visited Hawaii in 2000, the US government had recently decided that native Hawaiians, stripped of their rights and land in 1898, had no recourse to compensation, distinctly unlike their mainland Native American counterparts.

Let it be noted that none of the foregoing factual information comes from the Marxist guide to American imperialism. All of this can be found in the most conservative of history books. If you want to check that out, try *The Encyclopaedia of World History* by the American academics William Langer & Peter Stearns (published by James Clarke & Co., Cambridge).

What such books do not recount – for it is not their purpose – is the cult of territorial, military and economic imperialism which, for the past hundred years, has been hidden behind the plausible epithets about the US being the defender of freedom and protagonist for democracy. And where such exploits have not been hidden, they have been euphemised.

We may remember that when Reagan, president of a nation with 250 million inhabitants and the most buoyant economy in the world, felt threatened by the impoverished Nicaragua with around 3 million inhabitants, he said that he wanted Nicaragua to 'cry uncle'. This is a term often used by a school bully when he has some helpless child wriggling under physical restraint.

And we might remember that – whether in Iraq in past military incursions, or in Afghanistan in the present strife – although innocent lives are lost, the US never kills civilians. Dead non-military nationals are the vulgar synonyms for 'collateral damage'.

It might be salutary to consider one comment by a biased observer. Noam Chomsky has been rated by *The New York Times* as 'the greatest intellectual alive' and *The Chicago Tribune* rated him the eighth greatest intellectual in history just behind Plato and Sigmund Freud.

In one of his monographs, Chomsky notes how the Republican Party in the US is forever chastising the Democrats as being the party of 'special interests', by which is meant women, blacks, gays, old people – indeed society in general. Then, with hand on heart, they assert themselves to be the party of 'national interest' by which they euphemistically mean the interest of the business and financial sector, whose altruism is perennially being called into question.

UNDERSTANDING SEPTEMBER 11TH

Despite all this, and irrespective of the global and regional context, the vile nature of what happened on September 11th can never be excused, explained away or ameliorated. It was a damnable assault on innocent people.

But what I want to do now is to reflect on various perspectives on the disaster.

1. Entering the real world

The first is that it seems to me that September 11th was America's unwitting entrée into the real world. People who have seen American television or read US newspapers will know that other nations are mentioned in the main only when there has been a trade deal, a military coup involving US forces or a visit by the US president.

In November 2001, there was an interesting letter to *The Guardian* from a Sam Semoff from Liverpool in which he made the comment that the global view of the USA is illustrated by the fact that when the top two baseball teams play in the US, it is called the 'World Series'.

The language that has been extensively used with regard to incursions into other people's territory, economy or culture has been to do with 'America's interests', whether that be the expectation of unlimited oil from the Middle East or the import tax levied on foreign films – particularly from France – thereby safeguarding Hollywood from competition and the American people from a broader cinematic experience. What does not seem to have dawned on the USA is that other countries have legitimate national interests, some of which might include saying no to the imperialistic designs of the US, or offering a critique of American policy that is not fawning and congratulatory.

This fortress mentality and isolationism of the USA can be seen in the previous expectation of the US that the United Nations would back it whatever it did while, under the tutelage of Senator Jessie Helms, remaining unwilling to pay its dues to the UN until after September 11th.

Sadly, since then there has been no determination to broaden the world-view. More evident have been indications that isolationism is hardening – as may be deduced from the failure to ratify the Kyoto Accord on global pollution, and the threat to pull out of Nato if American troops became liable to prosecution for war crimes.

It seems that from an American perspective, there is only one solution to any foreign national or international problem, and that is America's solution, predicated always on a self-righteous and self-referential mentality, and blatantly ignorant of patterns of cultural or social polity which are as important to other nations as America's standards are to it.

To give just one example, anybody who has been in a Mediterranean souk or market place knows that in order to buy anything you have to strike a bargain. Earlier this year I was in Morocco and found myself looking at a rug which I half liked. Sufficient was my interest that the stall-holder began a long conversation about its virtues, leading to a recommendation that I should purchase it. So he told me the price, which was far too high, and there ensued ten minutes of haggling in which I assured him that I wasn't a wealthy tourist but a day visitor taking time out of a conference in Gibraltar.

After ten minutes I got the rug at 60% of the asking price, which was more than I ostensibly wanted to pay and less – ostensibly – than the trader wanted to sell it at. We both went away feeling that we had completed a transaction without either of us losing face. That is the way with Arab merchants.

Now, can you imagine some innocent housewife from Morocco, skilled in the bargaining systems of the bazaar, going into a supermarket in Boston. Supposing she gets to the checkout desk and the checkout operator says, 'That'll be $24.00,' in the full expectation that the shopper will pay by cash or credit card. Supposing instead the Moroccan woman says, 'I'll give you $12,' with the expectation that she might eventually have to part with four dollars more. Should such an exchange take place, the police would be called, and the Moroccan woman arrested for deception, while all the time she was exhibiting a different cultural understanding of shopping.

Writ large, this is part of the difficulty with the USA's understanding of Palestine, Iran, Iraq, Afghanistan and a dozen other Muslim nations. The language of diplomacy is not the same and an Eastern government will not enter into discussions with the USA if the negotiating game is going to be played according to American rules and therefore biased in the USA's favour.

It is interesting that, in launching his worldwide war on terror, Bush only very late in the day acknowledged that two of the first countries to offer unconditional help after September 11th were Australia and Canada. Equally late in the day he admitted to the almost immediate presence of senior British military advisers in Washington. The message to the world was that we were all united against terrorism; the message to the American people was 'We're doing this on our own.'

I believe that there is perhaps no more urgent issue facing the world as it deals with the USA than the need to broaden an introspective centre-of the-universe mentality into an integrated 21st century world-view.

2. The shambles of security

The second reflection on the events of September 11th has to do with the viability, in the 21st century, of a nation's defences, no matter how sophisticated, to deal with strategies of terrorism aimed not primarily at soldiers but at symbolic monuments of national self-confidence or at a nation's health and social infrastructure.

In another context entirely I have mentioned how if a husband and wife are arguing and she calls him an idiot and even throws a cushion or a cup in his direction, he may put it down to PMT or her temperament. But if she removes her wedding ring and flings it out of the window, the assault is much more profound.

And that was what happened on September 11th. It was not an occasion when American forces were locked in combat, where some might risk losing their lives in a theatre of war monitored by satellite. It was an incident which involved a city centre landmark and its occupants being annihilated by people who had no handguns in their pockets, let alone nuclear weapons at their disposal.

And the concomitant sabotaging of the mail system with anthrax spores being sent through the post – a riddle that has never been solved – exposed everyone, Britain included, to the possibility of urban guerrilla warfare becoming the terrorist tactic of the future in cosmopolitan communities where the loyalty of citizens to their country of residence cannot be guaranteed.

You cannot stop suicide bombers, just as you cannot stop reservoir polluters or people who put glass in milk bottles, by building ever more powerful military arsenals. For, with notable exceptions, the wars of the present and the potential wars of the future have or will have more to do with money than with territory, more to do with debt and indebtedness than with arsenals, more to do with the confusion caused by mega-corporations working transglobally, with accountability to no one but their shareholders, than to do with nation rising against nation.

At a time when the USA, which spends more on defence than the next four largest defence spenders in the world, has the military capability to wage war simultaneously in the Pacific and the Atlantic, the world's policeman on September 11th was shown to be like the emperor wearing no clothes. And it may just be, as former president Bill Clinton has stated, that the threat of further global terrorism will only be thwarted by a concerted effort to deal with the root causes of poverty, hunger and discrimination which force people to see violence as the language of the oppressed.

3. Feelings are not enough

The third comment I would like to make is that September 11th – as indeed Princess Diana's death two years previously – showed the dividing line between tragedy and entertainment to be lamentably thin.

I don't know how many times CNN showed the planes crashing into the World Trade Towers. It seemed as if the news was on a loop and could not come out of it. Then the addiction set in for pictures of people crying, people testifying to the horror of it all, people taking down the shell of the building, people standing to attention when the fragments of another fire-fighter's remains were removed, people writing messages on walls of paper in Penn Station.

We all have a fascination with destruction. It is what Erich Fromm calls necrophilia – an attraction to the decaying or disordered or dead. And if we become caught up in this fascination, as with pornography, we become inured to that which is mild and need to see something more nauseous, or to hear another testimony which will make us feel more horrified, as if simply by feeling we have either engaged with the tragedy or become part of the solution.

The awful thing for the camera about death is that it cannot film beyond it. It can only give an action replay of what led to this or that horror and this or that death, but the whetted appetite yearns for more of the same. This is particularly the case when you are dealing with a mystery. A straightforward, premeditated, anticipated killing does not engage our imagination. But when it is cloaked in mystery it provides morbid entertainment.

This was true of the way in which the nation responded to the deaths of the two young girls from Soham – Holly Wells and Jessica Chapman. It happened in a time and place that none would have predicted, for reasons that are not yet clear, and by people whose positive identification as the killers has not finally been established.

On one news programme, it was called the most horrible murder in our lifetime. I don't think so. What about Fred

West? What about Dr Shipman? What about the massacre of children at Dunblane? The difference is that these other killings were not so indelibly shrouded in mystery

There have been other events in the world in 2001 in which thousands of people have been killed by earthquakes, famines, floods, road accidents. But there has been nothing quite as mysterious, as unexpected, as inexplicable as September 11th.

The nature of the tragedy engages the imagination which, as when we read a detective novel, wants to conjecture and discover more. It becomes a morbid entertainment in which a society used to instant gratification cannot cope with the lack of clues or of progress.

Hence, perhaps, the push for the White House to announce strategy, to get troops mobilised, egged on by people like Senator John McCain who wrote soon after September 11th:

Only the complete destruction of international terrorism and the regimes that sponsor it will spare America from further attack.
(NB It wasn't attacked in military terms)

American military power is the most important part. When it is brought to bear in great and terrible measure, it is a thing to strike terror in the heart of anyone who opposes it. No mountain is big enough, no cave deep enough to hide from the full fury of American power.

The concentration on subjective and vengeful feelings is what I find most distressing about the post-September 11th scenario. It is as if the whole American nation is grieving not only for the loss of four thousand citizens but also for the non-existence of a political vocabulary with which to address, critique and respond to the tragedy.

Rather than deal with why the disaster occurred and what in America's engagement with the world could possibly have led to such a heinous crime, people have been locked into their own feelings. And when this introspection is encouraged or abetted by religious leaders or media pundits, any objective appraisal of the event is impossible.

I had a phone call from one of my friends in Chicago who was annoyed that I had not phoned him immediately in the wake of the tragedy. He felt I should have been checking that he was all right. I informed him that, to the best of my knowledge, the terrorist attacks never involved Chicago and that his native city was a thousand miles from any of the three incidents of that day. I then told him how Glasgow was less than two hundred miles from Belfast, but that I had not been aware when there was a bomb blast in Northern Ireland of his solicitation for my welfare. He was not amused.

Ironically, when I asked another friend who lives in New York how she had coped with the tragedy, she said that she was fed up with everyone asking. 'I live in the Bronx,' she said. 'What would I be doing walking about that rich neck of the woods in Manhattan?'

If there has been anything to commend in America's immediate response after September 11th, it must be that the little it has done has shown how misguided it would have been to do much more. The word in Ecclesiastes is very profound which says there is a right time. For to have acted on impulse and satisfied the public's craving for revenge whetted by personal feelings of threat or anger would have escalated global instability.

THREE BIBLICAL PARADIGMS

Lastly I want to offer some kind of biblical construct, although this is inevitably limited in its scope. And I have no doubt that people who have thought through the issue theologically may be aware of different reference points from those I will mention.

What I am not doing here is to offer proof texts or prophecies. The world – and certainly the US-centred world – has heard enough in the past 15 years from tele-evangelists like Pat Robertson and Jerry Falwell about how everything from the dismantling of the Iron Curtain to the Aids epidemic can be tied down to this or that verse of scripture.

I am not in that business. But what I am going to do is to offer what might seem like three unlikely paradigms which might help us to view the events of September 11th in a scriptural context. A paradigm, I repeat, is not a prophecy, but an example, a pattern of God's will, or of what happens in the world God made.

1. The tower

The first has to do with a tower. Not the tower of Siloam, which fell and killed innocent people and which Jesus used as an illustration of how disaster was not ordained by a malevolent

God, but the tower of Babel in the eleventh chapter of Genesis.

Why did the tower of Babel fall? Because it was faultily built, like the tower of Pisa? No. It fell because it was the result of people believing that they had a common language and should therefore build a monument to make a name for themselves.

It fell because the builders failed to respect the implanted differences that God had set in creation, not as fault lines, but as the means by which people and tongues could be differentiated, acknowledge each other's culture and not presume that they were all the same. Rather than respect these differences, the builders wanted to homogenise everything.

There is something uncanny about the twin towers because in them everyone – representatives of the variety of races in the world – spoke one language: the language of trade with a distinctly American accent. From there much global trade was organised. In the commodity market, New York speculators could decide the cost of coffee in Brazil which had not yet been planted, let alone harvested. And they made such decisions presuming that they would be acceptable outside the charmed circle of international traders, by those whose lands, cultures and livelihoods have been systematically ravaged by the avarice of the northern hemisphere's consuming classes.

I am not saying that Babel was a prophecy of September 11th, but it is a paradigm, an illustration of what one might expect to happen in God's world when an elite who think they have a global language build a proud monument to their ability, irrespective of those on whose bent backs and hard labour they ride.

~~And if I have to specifically expound this *vis à vis* the USA, I~~ would have to say that I do not believe it is the will of Almighty God, whose name appears on dollar notes, that 7% of humanity should dictate and decide how the other 93% live and respond to the self-appointed world guardians.

2. The wife

The second paradigm is also from the book of Genesis, and it too is an odd story which invariably embarrasses preachers and provides comic material for geologists.

It is the story in Genesis 19 of Lot and his wife and family fleeing from the city of Sodom which God had decided to destroy because its inhabitants were so inhospitable.

The apex of the story, to which Jesus himself alluded, is that Lot's wife, despite warnings to look only forward, looks back and turns into a pillar of salt. If it stretches your credulity or makes you wary of putting salt on your chips in case you thereby ingest Mrs Lot's DNA, that's your concern.

My concern is to see its paradigmatic value. What is the story about and why does Jesus tell us to 'remember Lot's wife'?

At the centre of the story is an express command: 'Don't look back.' On what? On the destruction that is behind you. Why not? Because in looking back there is a real possibility that you will become immobilised by it and develop an unhealthy interest in the problematic past rather than the potential of the future.

You and I know, from observing people who have the pictures of their deceased relatives staring at them from above the television, how true it can be that if you continually gaze on what has gone, you retreat into the past rather than walk into the future. This could become the negative experience out of which America lives, more intent on seeking revenge than in building alliances or entering into reciprocal partnerships with nations whose world view identifies the USA as the transgressor rather than the guarantor of liberties *vis à vis* a healthy ecosphere, and a landmine-free and debt-free southern hemisphere.

It is a sad reality that rather than the world's leading nation leading us anywhere, there has been virtually no positive, progressive movement initiated by the present US administration in matters of ecology, civil rights, world peace or amendment to the travesty of world debt. There has been, however, a great deal of self-indulgent retrospection and braying for revenge which does not secure global safety.

3. The fat king

The third paradigmatic story is one that few people may know, because not many find the book of Judges savoury reading material, especially the story of Ehud and Eglon in Chapter 3.

In brief, Eglon is a fat king who imposes his will and benefits financially from his ability to use his military and economic power to subjugate other countries, including the fledgling Israel. To save the Jews, God raises up Ehud, a left-handed man and therefore an untrusted outsider among his own people. Ehud takes the tax due to Eglon after securing a sword under the right-hand side of his tunic. After presenting the tax, Ehud asks to see the king in private, tells him that he has a message for him from God, whisks out his

~~sword with his right hand and sticks it through the fat king's~~
belly. Then he makes his escape and his people are freed of
the tyranny of their oppressor.

When I asked a group of church folk in Wales why that story
was in the Bible, I received the predictable range of replies.
But I had not expected the least likely of the well-dressed
brigade to say,

> *'It's there so that one day we will be able to talk about
> September 11th.'*

What he was alluding to was that, in the story, the wealth of
the fat king and the troops round his palace did not protect
him from being fatally wounded by the least likely of people –
a man who was left-handed.

This story does not cast the USA in the role of the evil king
(though a lot of its money is made from client nations) any
more than it suggests that the hijackers are heroes of biblical
proportions. But it does suggest that sometimes those people
who are most aggrieved by the misuse of one nation's power
may discover the subtlest and perhaps the simplest means by
which to injure its ego and deflate its pride.

NO NEAT CONCLUSION

There is no neat conclusion to this discussion, for this is not a
neat subject. So I am not going to end with a memorable
epigram or some clarion call to blind faith.

I'm going to end with the words of a song written in 1998
when the US and Britain decided for a second time to make

incursions into Iraq. Pray God, in the wake of September
11th may we not have to sing again:

If the war goes on
and the children die of hunger
and the old men cry
for the young men are no more;
and the women learn
how to dance without a partner,
who will keep the score?

If the war goes on
and the truth is taken hostage
and new horrors lead
to the need to euphemise;
when the calls for peace
are dismissed as sentimental,
who'll expose the lies?

If the war goes on
and the daily bread is terror,
and the voiceless poor
take the road as refugees;
when a nation's pride
destines millions to be homeless
who will heed their pleas?

If the war goes on
and the rich increase their fortunes
and the arms sales soar
as new weapons are displayed;
when a fertile field
turns to no-man's land tomorrow,
who'll approve such trade?

111

If the war goes on,
will we close the doors of heaven?
If the war goes on
will we breach the gates of hell?
If the war goes on
will we ever be forgiven?
If the war goes on ...

... and may God bless America.

* © WGRG, Iona Community, Glasgow G2 3DH, Scotland

10 In hope of heaven

Texts: Psalm 90; John 6:30–40

It is my Father's will that everyone
who sees the Son and has faith in
him should have eternal life; and I
will raise them up on the last day.

Saints and souls

A year ago, I was working in Sweden from late October to early November.

I had the Saturday off in Stockholm and was quite bemused by the sight of people going through the streets with bouquets of flowers and candles. I was even more bemused when I discovered that these were destined not for living rooms but for graveyards. In the churchyard of every ancient church in the city flowers were placed on the graves and large candles were lit.

Certain graves, like that of Olaf Palmer (the former Swedish premier who was assassinated in 1990), had more flowers than any other. Some people simply laid flowers, lit candles and went away. Others stood there in silence, thinking or praying or weeping. And in the evening, every church in the city was filled with people who had come to hear the Fauré *Requiem*, or the Brahms *Requiem*, or sacred choral music by Bach.

This happens every year when Sweden marks the crossover from October to November during the feasts of All Saints and

All Souls. Now, what are the feasts of All Saints and All Souls? you might ask. And the answer is quite simple.

All Saints is the time when the church remembers all those who have been canonised who don't have a special day to themselves. And All Souls is the day for remembering people who may not have been enrolled in the list of famous heroes of the faith, but whose life and witness have reflected the love of Jesus.

But another question – perhaps more pertinent to some – may be asked:

A FEAST FOR PROTESTANTS?

What has all this to do with us? – especially to Protestants who don't believe in saints but name our churches after them, especially to Protestants who know more about poor souls than about All Souls.

Well, what it has to do with us, irrespective of our religious affiliation, is that the only certainty in life is that we will die.

- We cannot be sure that we will win the lottery, even if we try it every week,
- we cannot be sure that we will become grandparents, even though our children are married,
- we cannot be sure that our scones will rise in a new oven, even though we have baked them a thousand times in the old.

But we can be certain of our death.

And yet, despite this certainty, it is the one reality we are hesitant to speak of, as if to speak of it is to hasten it on its way.

It is other people's deaths that concern us. In my case, this week, it was the father of a friend, and one of my colleagues who never woke up from his sleep, aged 37. It is other people's potential deaths that concern us as we watch other folk growing frail, or see someone making a slow recovery from surgery, or wonder if our friend who drives a lot will be safe on the roads.

But our own death ... our own death we don't contemplate through fear of being morbid, and certainly not much in the Protestant church.

Not for us the last rites,
not for us being laid up with ceremony in the church,
not for us incense billowing around our coffin
or water being sprinkled on it.

Not for us the commendation said by priest or people:

Receive her soul
and present her to God the most High.

Not for us even the first Wednesday in Lent as a time to remember our mortality.

(I remember a Methodist clergyman telling me of how on Ash Wednesday two years ago he was putting ash on the foreheads of his parishioners, among whom was a woman in her 80s who had had a very hard life. As he touched her brow, he said to her as he said to all the others:

From dust you came,
and to dust you shall return.

... to which she replied,

> *Thank God,*
> *oh thank God.)*

But I'm digressing. That's not for us. We're Protestants. We don't go in for that. We don't want to be reminded of our death. We don't go in for All Saints or All Souls. Hallowe'en and putting back the clock is as much as we can contend with as autumn turns into winter.

Be that as it may, I want to take advantage of this season to say two things about our death and one about those we love who have died.

DEATH IS TO BE FEARED NO MORE THAN BIRTH

If we could think ourselves back into the womb – though that takes a lot of thinking – we probably wouldn't have wanted to be born. As a foetus in the womb, we were warm, we were cared for, we were nourished, we were safe. As a foetus in the womb, we may occasionally have heard menacing noises from the next world, the world outside.

We may have conjectured that this next world was a frightening place, because we had never seen it, never been there. And if we had been told that after nine months we would emerge from this place of safety into the place of uncertainty and risk ahead of us, we might have said, 'No thank you. I'll just stay where I am.'

And as the moment of birth drew near, if we could have thought about it, wouldn't we have been apprehensive, sensing
the convulsions of pain around us,
the moaning of our mother,
the rapid movement from the ward to the birthing room,
the breaking of the waters in which we were safely cradled,
the journey down the birth canal into what would seem like eternal separation?

And then, though we never anticipated it, there were arms to hold us, and hands to caress us, and people we had never seen, but whose voices we had dimly heard, keen to welcome us into the world.

Oh yes, if we had the power to think in the womb we would not have wanted to be born. But having made that journey, from the familiar into the unknown, why need we fear death, surrounded as it also is with mystery and the fear of pain, and the apprehension of eternal separation?

Might it not be that when we come to make that last journey, as all the familiar things of this life are gradually taken from us, we emerge from the safety of what we know into greater life,
where there is greater security,
where there will be others to hold and welcome us,
and where we shall see face to face the one whose voice we have heard echoed here?

We should fear our death no more than we fear our birth.

WE SHOULD FEAR OUR DEATH NO MORE
THAN OUR BAPTISM

Christians should fear death no more than baptism, for our baptism is the sign of to whom we belong. It is not an insurance policy against injury in this life; it is a badge of our association with Jesus Christ.

We are part of his body, so intimately bound to him that whatever happened to him will also happen to us. Just as he died, so will we die, but just as he rose to life so all those who have been associated with him in his death will know the joy of resurrection.

It may seem to some a lot of nonsense that at the funeral of a Roman Catholic, the priest sprinkles the coffin with water. What is the point of that? we may ask. Well, I hope someone sprinkles water on my coffin when I die, not because it is a lucky charm, but because it is a reminder that at baptism water was sprinkled on us. We were baptised into membership of the body of Christ who died and rose again, so that, when we die, that badge of belonging will signify our rising to life on the great resurrection morning.

When I have travelled by air, waiting at a conveyor belt for my luggage, I sometimes see a case or cases going round and round and round with no one claiming them – perhaps because the owner has forgotten, perhaps because the luggage has lost its label. For me that is what hell is like, spinning around and around for ever because you have lost the sign of the one to whom you belong. And heaven is being brought into intimate contact with the One, part of whose body you are by the sign of water which was sprinkled on you at baptism.

We should fear our death no more than we fear our birth – and we should fear our death no more than we fear our baptism.

REMEMBERING THOSE IN HEAVEN

With the festivals of All Saints and All Hallows in mind, let me say one thing about those who have died, and from whom we may feel painfully separated.

About ten years ago, a man spoke to me at the General Assembly of the Church of Scotland in Edinburgh. I don't know who he was, apart from that he was an elder. And he told me a story about himself which was very touching in its honesty and simplicity.

He spoke of how, as a young man, he had gone out with a girl for two or three years. They were fond of each other, but they never made their way into marriage because they agreed that it wasn't for them. So their relationship ended, but they remained friends. The man – Andrew let's call him – married another girl, and 47 years later was still happily and devotedly married. But there was always in a corner of his heart a fondness for the first girl he had been serious about.

About two months before we met, this first girlfriend died, and when Andrew heard of her death he was quite distraught. He wished he had been able to say to her that she had always been important to him. He felt that he had never been able to say a proper goodbye. And now she was gone and he had to deal with an odd sense of frustration.

I asked him if he prayed, and he said he did. I asked him if he believed that his former girlfriend was with God in heaven and he said he did. I asked him if he believed that Jesus heard his prayers and would answer him in the right way and he said he did.

'Well then,' I said, 'why don't you ask Jesus tonight to tell your first girlfriend that you are remembering her, and ask him to tell her all the things that you wish you could have said before she died.'

... And Andrew looked as if somebody had handed him a million pounds. I wondered why 'reformed' faith had hitherto prevented this lovely man from trusting Jesus, his Saviour in heaven, to give Andrew's love to his friend

If we believe that those we have loved and lost are with God in heaven, and if we believe that Jesus hears our prayers, then we have in him one who can say to those we have loved and lost the things that mortality prevents us from saying, until in heaven we see him and them face to face ...

whether that is ... I'm sorry
or ... I forgive you
or ... I miss you
or ... I still love you.

This we can do with confidence because, though time and eternity are different realities to us, they are not to Jesus who, throned in splendour among the saints, still hears our cry as he shares the company of our friends and prepares a place among them for us.

STATES OF BLISS & YEARNING
The marks and means of authentic Christian spirituality
John L. Bell

Spirituality is not a permanent high, a continual blissed-out state. To experience the heights, one has also to know the depths. In this book based on speeches and sermons delivered in marquees, cathedrals and local churches, John Bell deals with issues as diverse as private devotion and public debt. The picture of God that emerges is not one of a 'celestial sadist' but rather a compassionate being who asks that we do only what we can, starting from where we are, to be just and compassionate too.

112 pp   ISBN 1 901557 07 3

THE SINGING THING
A case for congregational song
John L. Bell

A book for those who want to encourage others to sing, or to sing better. John Bell offers ten persuasive answers to the question 'Why do we sing?' Each chapter provides one answer, ranging from the straightforward ('because we can', 'to express emotion') to the more intriguing ('to revisit the past', 'to obey a command'). Each answer is explored with a wealth of illustration and practical insight born of the author's twenty years of experience in this field.

200 pp   ISBN 1 901557 28 6

JESUS AND PETER
Off-the-record conversations
John L. Bell & Graham Maule

These much-loved imaginary dialogues between Jesus and his eager disciple Peter are perfect as discussion-starters or scriptural reflections in small groups and church services or for personal reflection. In true Wild Goose Resource Group tradition, these scripts use completely up-to-date language and present a dynamic modern perspective on perennial issues such as faith, money, marriage, vocation, sex, healing, taxes, ecological concern, commitment, children, the kingdom of heaven, and much more.

128 pp   ISBN 1 901557 17 0

A WEE WORSHIP BOOK
Fourth incarnation
Wild Goose Worship Group

A collection of liturgies for morning, day, evening, Holy Communion and healing services, which has been used with enthusiasm by countless people, lay and clergy alike. Geared primarily for participative worship with shared leadership and includes optional methods of scriptural reflection and prayer with symbolic action. There is also a preface of comments on leading worship, dealing with all the issues which ordained clergy never tell lay people but presume they should know.

128 pp   ISBN 1 901557 19 7
Also available in a hardcover limited gift edition, bound with red cloth, with slipcase. Can be obtained only by mail order direct from Wild Goose Publications.

The Iona Community

The Iona Community, founded in 1938 by the Revd George MacLeod, then a parish minister in Glasgow, is an ecumenical Christian community committed to seeking new ways of living the Gospel in today's world. Initially working to restore part of the medieval abbey on Iona, the Community today remains committed to 'rebuilding the common life' through working for social and political change, striving for the renewal of the church with an ecumenical emphasis, and exploring new, more inclusive approaches to worship, all based on an integrated understanding of spirituality.

The Community now has over 240 Members, about 1500 Associate Members and around 1500 Friends. The Members – women and men from many denominations and backgrounds (lay and ordained), living throughout Britain with a few overseas – are committed to a fivefold Rule of devotional discipline, sharing and accounting for use of time and money, regular meeting, and action for justice and peace.

At the Community's three residential centres – the Abbey and the MacLeod Centre on Iona, and Camas Adventure Camp on the Ross of Mull – guests are welcomed from March to October and over Christmas. Hospitality is provided for over 110 people, along with a unique opportunity, usually through week-long programmes, to extend horizons and forge relationships through sharing an experience of the common life in worship, work, discussion and relaxation. The Community's shop on Iona, just outside the Abbey grounds, carries an attractive range of books and craft goods.

The Community's administrative headquarters are in Glasgow, which also serves as a base for its work with young people, the Wild Goose Resource Group working in the field of worship, a bi-monthly magazine, *Coracle*, and a publishing house, Wild Goose Publications.

For information on the Iona Community contact:
The Iona Community, Fourth Floor, Savoy House,
140 Sauchiehall Street, Glasgow G2 3DH, UK. Phone: 0141 332 6343
e-mail: ionacomm@gla.iona.org.uk; web: www.iona.org.uk

For enquiries about visiting Iona, please contact:
Iona Abbey, Isle of Iona, Argyll PA76 6SN, UK. Phone: 01681 700404
e-mail: ionacomm@iona.org.uk